"BELIEVE"

DEALING WITH JOB SEARCH STRESS AND PREPARING FOR A JOB SEARCH IN AN IMPERFECT WORLD

M. B. BLACKER

"believe"

Dealing with Job Search Stress and Preparing for a Job Search in an Imperfect World

2020 - 2021© – All Rights Reserved

All rights reserved. No part of this book may be reproduced, in any form or by any means, or stored in a database or retrieval system, without ***explicit acknowledgement of the source, author and annotations of sources represented in this publication, and notification of the author of any intention to utilize this material.*** Any other type of copying or reproduction of the materials in this publication is prohibited by copyright laws. In the job paradigm of today's job search, materials and techniques are in constant flux, and it is the belief of the author that this material should be made available to those seeking assistance.

I have been careful to provide accurate information in this book, but it is possible that errors and omissions have been introduced. In addition, all materials from additional referenced sources have been annotated to the best of my ability with no intentional errors or inaccuracies. Sources were notified for permission for the use of quoted and noted materials to the best of my ability to avoid copyright infringements while preparing this book. Any purchaser of this book shall hold harmless the author for any materials or omissions as noted within this section or book materials.

All brand names and product names used in this book are trade names, service marks, or registered trademarks of their respective owners and are subject to applicable laws and regulations.

CONTENTS

Preface	v
Introduction	xi
1. How Attitude, Stress and Anxiety Impact Your Job Search	1
2. Attitude: How to Define, Build, and Manage it for the Job Search	22
3. Stress: How to Manage it in the Job Search	43
4. Managing Time and Controlling Stress Factors	61
5. Effective Communication in the Job Search	82
6. Developing a Positive Marketing	102
7. Positive Tools, Methods, and Techniques for a Productive and Positive Interview Experience	134
8. What's Next and How to be Prepared for the Long & Short-Term "Gig" Economy	177
9. Living and Surviving Pandemics, Recessions, And Other Economic Chaos	189
Notes	197

PREFACE

I first began to put this book together in early 2020 for the job search issues relating to stress and how to manage this emotional situation in your job search. Now as we are in the fourth quarter of 2020 and first quarter of the year 2021 and facing a global pandemic, the world of work has changed more drastically than in the Great Depression of the early part of the twentieth century, several depressions and the Great Recession of 2008 that followed in the twenty-first century. Whether you want to accept it or not, the world of work has changed, will change more, and will take at least the next several years to "correct" itself to a more stable status.

As I reedit and modify this book for job seekers, I have added sections to assist you with managing a job search during these times. ***Believe*** is still centered around you, just in more ways now than over the last twelve months.

The Great Pandemic of 2020 will change work as you think you know and understand it. Approximately 30% to 45% of technology, customer service, customer support, and other services will no longer be based in an external, centralized office location. Workers will be working from their home office for at least a year or more. Job descriptions will change, responsibilities will be modified, and requirements will be redesigned. Adapting to change will be the first and most challenging behavior for the foreseeable future. Stress and anxiety of the job search, even while working, will grow!

You must now realize the job search continues to be an ever-changing paradigm. Even though unemployment rates were at their lowest in several decades and compensation continues to lag, work itself as we currently understand it has changed. It is a greater changing paradigm, in and of itself. Part-time, contractual, and temporary work and multiple sources of income is the new paradigm for this decade and perhaps beyond. In addition, there is a forced change between the balance of work and other external and internal relationships, such as family, acquaintances, friends, activity involvement, and a host of other activities that one could take for granted just a few years ago. The Great Recession of 2008 has changed our daily life in many ways. Most affected is the importance of attitude and stress management for the job seeker.

As a job seeker, you must not only learn and understand these new paradigms but develop the capability and capacity to manage what affects you, such as the new work paradigm, career development, the job "continuing" search paradigm, and the successful and effective management of attitude and stress. This activity is vital for all generations of job seekers from the Millennial to the Baby Boomer and recent college graduates who are a mix of the end of the Millennial generation and the beginning of Generation Z. Although each generation deals with the job search in a different way, the end results will always be affected by how the job seeker manipulates the changes in paradigms.

Since 2008 I have worked with over two hundred job seekers who have sought reemployment. Although the methods I have shared and utilized with my clients and others may not have achieved the exact reemployment an individual desired, it did successfully provide new reemployment that will lead to greater opportunities in the future. Over the last five years, I have been a guest resume expert for several national and regional job search events assisting all generations of job seekers. I developed new methods for the Boomer job seeker that have been considered "out of the box" and have proven successful for scores of clients. In 2010 I opened a small firm that dealt with job search issues for the Baby Boomer generation, and my efforts continue to serve that generation. This book is written for all generations of job seekers because these issues are faced by all job searchers and must be effectively managed to attain job search success. My firm was originally started with the objective of providing the best and most up-to-date techniques and methodologies for the Boomer job seeker. Today our emphasis is assisting all job seekers in the job search arena.

Attitude and stress can and do play a significant role in the success of the job search. These factors of emotional behavior can and do act as a primary determination of being seriously considered for a potential job opportunity. The ability to recognize that a job seeker may have the best "work" experience and qualifications is no longer the sole key to job search success and meaningful reemployment. More and more employers are seeking not just the candidate's skills, abilities, accomplishments, cultural acceptance, and communication skills, experience and training, but also the need for a positive attitude that is expressed in the job seeker's personal marketing materials, the interview process, and many other aspects of the job acquisition process. In addition, adaptability has become a key factor in hiring today and that characteristic is measured by a candidate's attitude and the effects of stress on the job seeker.

Attitude is reflected in the job candidate by the "direct expressions," or the candidate's actions in the job search. As a job seeker, do you understand that your actions in the interview, from body language to the spoken answers you provide to an interviewer, from the presentation of your resume to other personal marketing materials, all reflect your attitude? Your attitude is revealed during every aspect of your job search, from the first step of developing your personal marketing materials, through the interview process, and even during the probationary period once you gain employment. A simple fact is this: your attitude is reflected as mentioned, but stress is also reflected in how you deal with attitude. This book is designed to assist you in managing attitude, controlling and managing stress, and learning key methods to maintain a healthy and positive attitude through adaptability and behavior modification actions in your job search process, especially in stressful situations that require stress management.

INTRODUCTION

The job search process today continues to be challenging and constantly changing in approach, positions, and opportunities every eighteen to twenty-four months. In other words, the job search process is an ever-changing paradigm, and the ability to understand it, cope with it emotionally, realistically, and most of all, effectively is an ongoing process. The new paradigm of work initiated by the Great Recession of 2008 has been and will continue to be ***changing!*** The process now involves not just understanding the new methodologies and technologies of the job search, but also dealing with the emotional and psychological impact of the total process. How to emotionally solve this process and complete it in a successful, confident, and time-oriented fashion will bring the job seeker of today the best possible results.

Looking back to when the Great Recession of 2008 hit the U.S. economic system, job seekers relied upon older methods for the job search. For the most part, these older methods are now outdated and fail to consider the more vital factors of the search. Today job seekers must not only understand the new methodologies but also the new technologies and the ever-changing paradigms for work, job seeking, and career maintenance. Yet most of all, job seekers of today must be able to adapt to the emotional and psychological aspects of the search. Stress management has become the key issue in surviving and succeeding in today's job search. It is extremely important to learn and utilize successful processes to make the process healthier and more effective, manageable, rewarding, and fulfilling.

The economy continues to affect workers today. According to the Bureau of Labor Statistics January 2014 report, 9.4% of the workforce is still underemployed and not much changed from those figures by mid-2018. This situation leads workers to lesser paying, lower responsibility positions or part-time work. Best estimates of the percentage of workers who ceased looking for work is now forecasted as 4% to 6% of the workforce. This suggests that although the BLS has reported the latest average unemployment rate at around 4.0%, the actual total of unemployed and underemployed represent around 10% to 12% of the available workforce. These numbers have never been this high for such a long period of time since the Depression of 1929, and fulfilling employment has not been at such low percentages since the 1970s. This pandemic has increased the rate of unemployment at an overall rate of 15% plus and we have no idea as to where it will go on a month-to-month basis.

INTRODUCTION xiii

In 2020 and for the foreseeable future, there is only one primary statement that talks directly to jobs: "JOBS CONTINUE TO BE AND ARE TEMPORARY and ACCEPTING THAT FACT WILL IMPROVE YOUR CAREER DEVELOPMENT, YOUR JOB SATISFACTION AND OVERALL LIFE-WORK BALANCE." Job seekers of any generation—Z, Millennial, X-Gen, or even Boomer—will face many similar stress-inducing problems. Each generation must deal with stress in successful and effective ways to develop coping tools, managing skills, and networking support methods that are necessary for the job search, mental health balance, and parallel life activities such as family and social activities.

Although a large percentage of job seekers recognize that there are changes, many are reluctant to fully understand how to successfully deal with these changes. To control stress factors, job seekers must develop necessary job tools, attain emotional support to reduce stress and anxiety, and change any negative thoughts to a more consistent positive outlook and viewpoint overall.

Let's be quite honest about jobs today! The former internet website "Careerrealism.com," now known as "workitdaily.com" had a perfect quote that all job seekers and career changers must fully remember: "***All jobs are temporary.***" Whether job seekers fear that statement or accept it depends on how they understand the true meaning of the statement. It is a well-known fact for job seekers, underemployed workers, and even those who have given up seeking work for now that the real unemployment numbers are well above the latest reported by the U.S. Bureau of Labor Statistics. The number of those who have "stopped" looking for work is still rather stagnant or may again be on the incline based on current economic policies. According to multiple articles, career opinions, and corporate, state, and federal reports, almost three-quarters of all jobs are part time or temporary with lower wages and with little or no benefits. In addition, another factor included in that employment number is related to those workers who are considered "contractual" and are recycled into the unemployed at the termination of the contract. On the brighter side, there is a ray of hope in several areas even today. The fields of health care and technology are showing some growth; however, the sustainability of that growth will depend upon the economy as a whole.

This does not mean you will not achieve success in your job search efforts. Although the length or period of time for the job search has grown from six months to a year as a generalized statement, many job seekers are in the process for well over a year before achieving success. In many instances, the more advanced in a career field, the longer the job search. Senior Executives are seeking employment rehire after periods of twelve to twenty-four months or longer and entry-level positions are generally six months or more. When you understand how to manage stress and its effects on your job search process, from your personal marketing to relationships, you can attain the success you desire with more meaningful results. The process requires hard work and planning and how to manage the stress that comes along with that is covered in this book.

Job seekers have a misconception that if one simply develops "quality" self-promoting marketing materials, practices interviewing skills, and uses various networking techniques, the chances for job acquisition will become a quick and easy reality. In one sense, that may be true. Yet in another, your attitude and your management of stress and anxiety do show through to prospective employers. You as a job seeker may not at first recognize this vital point, but it is a major component of this book. Of course the emphasis is how to do this in a positive and successful manner.

I've written and titled this book "believe" because this simple but unique word will express to you as a job seeker that all one does and achieves in the job search is based upon your own "belief system" as it relates to who you are. Your system may be based upon today's world of pop psychology, faith, meditation practices, spiritualism, and many other sources. I am certainly not condemning anyone's belief system about themselves, unless it is negative and produces negative life results. Every one of these belief systems is valid. Their validity is derived from developing a new mindset to give you, the perfect job seeker, the perspective necessary to achieve a positive emotional outlook for success, reduce stress and anxiety, and establish support mentors or groups, with the aim of assisting you in your job acquisition and life balance during that period.

Additionally, this book is titled "believe" because each letter in the word stands for the seven aspects of developing methods for managing stress, anxiety, and self-esteem and establishing positive strategic personal marketing materials to support a positive job search result—in other words, to maintain a healthier outlook in your job acquisition process and bring you job success. So let's analyze what each letter of the title will uncover for you in this book:

> **"b"** - The letter "b" is your **belief** in yourself, easy to say yet more difficult to practice. This is critical today. As humans losing a job is as difficult as losing a loved one, a close family member, or friend. It elicits guilt, anger, and even self-judgment of one's work skills and ability. Why else would you be terminated or laid off?
>
> As an individual who has lost their "means of livelihood," income, sustenance, or whatever term one may use, I believe it all boils down to this: the development of self-doubt. You were doing your job as a respected and valued employee, and the next moment you were informed that for some unknown or known reason you were no longer needed! Although most of the time it is not your fault, it was the economy, a major or minor management change, corporate restructuring, right-sizing, or realignment of the company's business, but in reality it may have been you that caused the loss of your position!

Yes, you have read this correctly. In many cases it was your fault, for any single or a multitude of reasons, correctly or incorrectly, that you are not currently in your in last position because of all of the reasons noted above, as well as your estranged "belief system." You may have worked yourself out of a job by establishing new and more efficient processes or methods to make your employer more efficient. Also, you may have failed to recognize that the temporary position was temporary or even that your position was one to determine what your employer hired you to do in reality, or even more simply, the position was contractual with a set time span to complete a specific project. Finally, you may not have been a "cultural" match for the current employer, a team player in a sense, and your adaption to it was not realistic. It could even be a point that you simply took your last position because you needed a "job" for survival.

Your self "belief system" is more important to you as a job seeker than you might have initially considered. This belief system is an issue that we are dealing with in this book, along with the other points as they relate to the job search.

> **"e"** - The letter "e" is representative of your self-**esteem**. Though closely related to self-worth, self-esteem is closer to the understanding that your accomplishments presented by you to an employer are "who you really are," not who you were as you interviewed or "appeared" during the interview process. Many job seekers view "belief" as the same

as self-esteem in work, and that is not an accurate portrayal. **Self-esteem** is an inward evaluation of the "total you": how you performed in your last job, how you honestly viewed your contributions to an employer, and more vital, how your employer viewed your contributions with or without acknowledgement. Self-esteem is related to the job seeker as one that categorizes how your performance in your work was accepted mentally by you and outwardly by your manager or the organization.

You might have a great "belief system" in yourself in practice, though your "work/personal self-esteem" may be just the opposite. This factor can also be caused by many reasons that include an analysis that you did not fit into the organization, your skill sets were superior or inferior to others on your team, and appropriate appreciation was never provided as feedback for you. But, here is the catch for understanding this as a new or existing job seeker: ***It doesn't matter any longer how you were perceived by your former employer; that employer WAS NOT and IS NOT you!*** However, the employer may have developed a perception of who you were based upon your production ability on the job. Any employer's perception is ***subjective***, so that may have lead to your status as a job seeker.

"**l**" - The letter "l" refers to **learning** and utilizing better methods in coping with the job search process. This is relevant to establish new methods in adapting to the stress of the job search and its effect on you. Stress is a component in the job search, and not managing it effectively is the most significant factor for failure to regain employment. This statement is relative because stress is presented in every aspect of your job search, from development of your personal marketing materials to your family relationships and social activities.

Many job seekers have attended various workshops, seminars, job clubs, career counselor sessions and meetings to learn the latest methods used for today's job search and acquiring relevant employment. As a resume writer specializing in the job search for the fifty plus, I have taught many job seekers new and innovative methods to be successful in the job acquisition process. It was not until early in 2016 did I realize that training to deal with the all-inclusive "stress" factors of the job search was equally vital to success and very little had been written to assist job seekers on this issue.

In the job market of today, it is necessary for the job hunter to compartmentalize the learning of the newest methods and technologies for a successful search and the most effective and affective processes in dealing with and managing stress. As job loss is generally recognized as an individual's second greatest factor to affect relationships of family, understandably these are vital. Understanding and management are crucial behavioral processes for stress management. Stress causes isolation, from all these groups mentioned. Job seekers begin to exhibit an inability to manage time, events, relationships, finances, and a host of other everyday activities. Learning and utilizing methods to manage stress and the job process is your number one priority as a job hunter.

"i" - Simply stated, the "**I**" is YOU! You are not what you think or who you think you are today or yesterday. Confusing but true, you are what you are planning to be tomorrow and each day afterward. If one understands Einstein's theory of time, time does not really exist; everything we do is happening at the same time, just in different or parallel universes. In this theory, everything you want to do and be, every positive attitude you want or have already exists, and that means you have a positive attitude as part of you. The difference is that you must develop it to utilize it to your advantage. In a parallel universe that new job already exists for you and you are in that position. This may be somewhat difficult for many to accept, but once you grab on to this concept, it will assist you in maintaining a positive attitude when dealing with stress issues. However, for the majority of us who are not physicists, as a job seeker you must "rebuild," regain understanding, and accept that you are a qualified job seeker. You can become what you plan about, what you think about, and what you act on. Some may consider this meta-physics, but it is a reality of life now!

Behavior modification is a very simple example of this process. Using the example every time you submit your personal marketing material to a prospective employer, you modify and improve your presentation. As results vary, you restructure based upon those results, which will lead you to the first successful part of the process, the initial interview, or a valid networking contact(s) with a reference resource for you. After more honing of your materials by using behavior modification evaluations, you redo your presentation materials to lead to more interviews, follow-up interviews, and finally to a successful job offer. Each step leads to what can be classified as behavior modification, causing you to improve your job search process by attaining greater reactive results.

As a job hunter and even as an employed, underemployed, or an individual who has dropped out of the job search for a while, it is important to understand the "I" that is you. Each job seeker working through the job search process is not what you are (your self-esteem alone), unless you want to remain in that state! Successful job acquisition requires action. It requires planning for tomorrow in a positive set of behavioral actions and the ability to have a "mental picture" of what you seek. Many job searchers that I have worked with state emphatically that "tomorrow" or "next month" they will have regained employment—yet their mental planning, which includes stress management, is not complete and leads to delayed success gratification. This mindset is generally known as a "feeder" for more and continued stress.

Thinking about the future in undefined terms and without planning, and of the job acquisition process in "hopeful" but unrealistic terms nullifies your job search process and contributes to the continuation of unmanageable stress and delayed job acquisition success. The result is longer job search periods, continual unmanaged stress, damage to relationships with others and those who can assist you in your efforts, and emotional and mental issues.

Finally the "I" represents a new thinking process forcing you to redefine what you want, when you want it, and how to view the process to develop your personal marketing tools for a more positive job search and successful results. Remember, this is not "pop" psychology this is straight behavioral action, it has a two thousand year historical process that can be traced back to the New Testament of the Bible. In the New Testament, it states in a very simplistic form the following: ask for what you need, believe with your "soul", "spirit", "proper mental attitude", "within your mind" that you will achieve and receive it, and "act", in a deliberate manner, as if you have already have it. This is what the planning process is all about.

> **"e"** - The second "e" in "believe" relates to **energy**. It is evident from the many clients that I have worked with that with each passing month of the job search, energy begins to drain more and more. For many job seekers, energy drains to the point that the job seeker has stopped the job search altogether. Stress is the killer of energy for the job hunter and stress will

cause the job seeker to extinguish the search either for a short period of time or for long periods of time. In some cases, stress will force the job seeker to stop looking for years! For those who have dropped out of the job search process, there are many more underlying factors along with stress that may require professional assistance.

The "employment reality" which shows a mixed status in the unemployment numbers fails to consider the reality of the "emotional unemployment situation." A large portion of this is due to the related loss of energy, from frustration and "stress out" mental fatigue. The necessity to utilize and adapt methods to maintain energy as you proceed to develop a successful job search is the key to gaining job acquisition.

"v" - The "v" stands for **victory**. Although all the topics relayed in this introduction are included in the book, including developing your job search personal marketing tools, the results must produce a victory. Victory is more than just acquiring a new job. Victory is a measurement of "your process," your ability to first understand then develop the required positive marketing materials, manage visible, unexpected, or unrecognized stress along with anxiety. In addition, to attain victory the job hunter must understand and accept in all respects the new job paradigms. Secondly, victory is the ability to maintain a positive balance between work and your personal family life activities. Third, victory is the acceptance that in the new work paradigms, all jobs are temporary, whether you are a "Boomer," "X-Gen," or "Millennial," and let's not forget those "Gen Z."

Victory relates to the job seeker's ability to continue to be prepared for the ever-changing paradigm of work. Some experts state that the work paradigm may change again within the next twenty-four months. Being prepared will prevent the effects of stress affecting your life and work. Maintaining all that you will learn will provide you with the proper compass direction not only for now, but for the future.

"**e**" - Finally, the last "e" in the word represents the **elite understanding**, the control, and the knowledge of who you are as an individual as an important asset to any prospective employer, but most of all, what your true values represent. Understanding and ACCEPTING that no matter what occurs with your acquisition of work, you will be able to control your job search processes. You will be able to manage stress and anxiety effectively and in a healthy manner, build your personal marketing materials, and balance the necessary time and commitment for work, family, friends, and other relationships.

Now that you understand the underlying premise of this book and how it came to be entitled "believe," it opens another path to utilize the job seekers' skills and experience to achieve a successful process. In the new job search process, change will always be inevitable. Each chapter in this book relates to the title of the book and the meaning behind each letter. Those topics although centering on all job seekers are as relevant to Boomers, X-Gens, Millennials, and Generation Z. Each chapter in this book is also relevant to managing your everyday life while in the job search process, relationships, stress, and the process itself.

1
HOW ATTITUDE, STRESS AND ANXIETY IMPACT YOUR JOB SEARCH

Every job seeker faces attitude shifts from positive to negative and from negative to positive. Job seekers face stress from long periods of unemployment, underemployment, family and work balance, finances, children who want everything now, and the list can go on and on. Anxiety is the result of attitudinal changes, the inability to understand and manage stress, and difficulty maintaining the best attitude for your job search process. The results are convoluted job search activities, longer periods of unemployment or underemployment, and a constant flux of attitude that affects every aspect of the job seeker's life, including family, friends, and especially the job seeker's self-value. The ability to learn and understand how to control, modify, develop, implement, and reinforce methods to deal with these issues is crucial for a successful job search.

Have you ever heard the statement that it takes ten positive points to overcome just one negative action? It has been found through multiple studies that although positive attitudes, feelings, and emotions are much more effective in life than negative ones, overcoming negativity is your priority task and challenge. This cannot be done overnight obviously, or in a day, a week, a month, or even several months. You can begin to build a lasting set of the necessary skills and methods to deal with this negativity over these time frames. However, it is an ongoing and continuous process. Understanding the processes and how to utilize them in your job search is the emphasis of this book. The information presented is only one small part of several major processes that compose the psychological aspect of attitude and personal outlook, stress management, and avoidance of anxiety.

As a job seeker, you don't need to understand the theories of psychology and sociology or the science behind communication, but you do need to understand and develop tools to overcome negative attitudes that produce stress and anxiety.

You need to learn methods that will:

......allow you to control and maintain a positive attitude for a positive job search.

......how to deal with everyday challenges that face the job seeker and affect your daily attitude.

......understand how your attitude, stress, and the resulting anxiety are related to each other.

......how to eliminate self-defeating behaviors when overwhelming factors attack your attitude.

......how to plan and implement an individualized plan to relieve stress-producing behaviors.

......understand and accept that only you, and you alone as the job seeker, can control your attitude.

......accept what is reality and what is not.

......accept that stress exists and how to effectively reduce its source.

......accept that stress DOES exist, even for the most qualified job candidate and placing stress in its proper perspective.

Most of all, however, you must be able to develop your job search tools, establish appropriate methods that will benefit you in your activities, and plan your search while dealing with attitude effects, stress producers, and the potential of anxiety. This book is divided into two categories designed to assist you first in understanding attitude, stress, and anxiety in the job search and secondly the new "nitty gritty" part of developing your "Personal Marketing Tools" for the job search. That means establishing a new style of job search planning, the "new" use of up-to-date materials that are relevant for job seekers. Yet the information included within this material will "reinitiate" older and proven methods to manage stress and anxiety. How to manage attitude, stress, and anxiety, as well as other factors, affects all job seekers, from Boomers to X-Gens to Millennials, and even the new Generation Z. These factors affect how job seekers "plant" their job searches in fertile soil where they are able to successfully grow, and then they utilize job search tools when seeking employment and even how they leave a job for a new opportunity. The point is that all job hunters are affected by these job search killers.

When you think about attitude, you might think about your household pet, the cat or the dog. These pets have "attitude." When you first received your pet, think about how you named the animal. In reality that name was a reflection of the critter's attitude. Names such as Missy, Prissy, Chubs, Princess, Butch, and so on, reflect the attitude that you observed in your pet's behavior when you first brought it home. Most times these names were quite appropriate for the animal and perhaps not even close to the real character of Princess or Butch as your pet grew older and their personalities developed from genetics and socialization. Pets are an excellent reflection of us and how we view ourselves in the mirror. If you are honest with yourself, you cannot deny that fact. We develop a reflection of our attitude in the same way. In our microcosm of our world, we either accept our attitudes or we deny them.

Attitudes, positive or negative, have a strong impact on your job search success. The same as how you establish a relationship with your pet. A self-defeating attitude, in other words, promotes a negative action that will stop your job search cold. As you will read in later chapters, you will learn ways to redevelop a positive attitude, how to maintain an attitude that is beneficial to your job search, and how to keep the effects of negative attitudes from defeating your job search process.

Peter Vogt[1], contributing editor to Monster.com, presents a generalized set of statements that are "to the point" on how your attitude can affect your job search. Although these are generalized in concept, they do show how your attitude affects the success of your job search. As is pointed out in this short summary, these attitudes cross all generations of job seekers.

> -**ENTITLEMENTS**- Many job seekers, Millennials, Gen-Xers, and Boomers, believe they "deserve" a good job! That attitude derives from the simple fact that a job seeker went to school, graduating with a high school diploma, college certificate, college undergraduate degree, graduate degree, technical certification, etc. They may have developed a false sense of what "schooling" or even "experience" is about or what it will provide. Although you have earned a

higher education or completed a technical skill training program, that is an accomplishment and a job seeker should recognize that fact. There may be even some employers who will reward you for that accomplishment above and beyond the "normal" skills, but I honestly doubt that. This is an important yet painful realization for many job seekers. Employers today want to see from candidates the ability to be solution providers.

A prospective employer will concur that you have a degree or years of experience, but so what? How many other candidates offer these same qualifications? So what happens, poof! All of a sudden your high spirits, the positive attitude you had when you first lost your position, the attitude you think you nourish daily to keep it positive falls flat on its face. The notion that entitlement alone makes you deserve to be hired is a non-reality for today and for the future decade to come, or perhaps longer. If your attitude is not positive to project the facts to support your education, your experience, your problem-solving abilities, your knowledge of an employer's needs and problems, you will have a difficult time in your job search. You will be no different than any other potential candidate in the field.

Younger or less experienced workers or highly experienced Boomers often feel entitled when they first lose their job. The belief that entitlement will get you a part-time position no longer holds true in the paradigm for work today. There are just too many job seekers today competing for the available full-time, part-time or other work opportunities, regardless of the latest open employment positions stated by the Bureau of Labor Statistics in September 2018. In addition, many of these job seekers fail to posses the required updated skills. This is most felt now in 2020, the year of the Pandemic!

-**LACK OF FOCUS**- Confusion is a common state of mind for all job seekers. This is a natural occurrence, especially during the first two to four weeks after losing a job. Unemployed job seekers are now receiving unemployment benefits of some type, perhaps still receiving a severance package, or even doing some part-time work. Although there may be times where attitude may become negative, as long as there is some definitive income it is not the issue. But IT WILL BECOME SOON!

Many job seekers are faced with typical questions: *What do I do now? What effect is that having on my attitude? Do I want a new career? I know it is only going to be a short time to get reemployed, or maybe not!* I've talked to many job seekers who even after a short period of unemployment will reply about regaining employment that they "will take anything they can get"! These are all valid emotional aspects of how the job seeker's attitude is affected in the work paradigm for today. In my work with over hundreds of job seekers, these are the most common statements that I hear. In reality, what the individual job seeker is saying is that "I don't the have the proper attitude to focus on what direction I need to take."

To a prospective employer, this negative attitude and the actions that the job seeker represents is viewed by employers as a lack of focus, confidence, and a non-positive mind set. One way an interviewer will react to this is by cutting the interview short or by telling the interviewee that something has "come up" or simply some excuse to end the interview. One important point I want to emphasize is that the more negative attitude that you keep bottled within, the more those negative attitudes will be expressed in all aspects of your job search.

-**"GIVE ME A BREAK"**- This was part of the "very old style" of the job search, from the 1970s, 1980s, and even carried over into the early 1990s. So many job seekers would ask for an opportunity to "show an employer what skills and experience they can demonstrate." A job seeker would volunteer to work for free or as an apprentice to try and present their commitment and skills to what they can do for an employer. As the economy and work have changed, this thinking that you are not valued by the lack of getting a chance still does have some merit. Today the idea of offering your services for free detracts from your value and your emotional state. However, volunteering in related opportunities in the community, non-profits, and other sectors are key in supporting your efforts. Doing this will also provide you with establishing a grounding and more uplifting attitude.

Prospective employees are, as an old adage states, "a dime a dozen" today. The fact that there are more potential employees than there are available positions needs to be understood! Employers care little about meeting an employee's needs. Even with all the current unfilled positions, the issue is that there are not enough trained employees to fill those positions. Employers care more about a candidate's abilities to solve their problems than about what each hire or action in a business will do to affect the bottom line. Although in the corporate environment problem-solving is prime, the issues that hinder a company are no longer secondary. Think about it: If problems that affect the bottom line remain unsolved in a company, then profitability is lost and jobs aren't needed!

The demand by stock holders, investors, venture capitalists, and loan institutions have placed the position of where an employee is viewed, regardless of what a company may say in its internal and external public releases. As previously stated, employers who are seeking to hire a qualified candidate for an open position have these main concerns: what that employee will do for me, how long I will need that employee, and what it will cost, as it relates to the net profit of the business operation versus overall costs of overhead staff.

As a job seeker, stop thinking about how YOU deserve a job. Millions of unemployed, underemployed, and part-time workers have this emotional mindset, and it must be modified for YOUR successful job search. Instead, concentrate on being the solution to a need for that employer. Develop a positive attitude and successful personal marketing approach that portrays a job candidate that an employer NEEDS TO HIRE! Establish within your positive attitude a mental picture of successfully competing in any interview situation, offering the best abilities to provide successful resolution to an employer's needs, and communicate that you know how to solve those needs better than any other candidate.

Learn to think like an employer. Understand the attitudes that are expressed in the interview process and you will have a head start over any other job seeker for any position.

Anger, Despair, Frustration Many job seekers who have been in the market for a period of time begin to feel anger, bouts of despair, and periods of depression. Although each of these feelings may change in their level of intensity, they are a normal part of behavior. They are part of the grieving process from the loss of work. These are natural feelings, but they are also behaviors that can produce self-destructive actions. There are several ways to deal with this when it becomes less manageable than you want.

..... recognize the issues that are causing your anger, despair, and frustration. Talk to a family member about what you are feeling and others who are working with you in the job search. Ask them how you are being perceived in their eyes.

..... if necessary, find professional help. There is professional help that is available free or at minimal cost. It is vital to your health and successful job search that you are in a healthy frame of mind for this important task.

This topic will be discussed more in Chapter Two.

In the meantime, remember these important points as a guide to dealing with stresses that will affect your attitude:

1. Learn to like yourself. That's correct: learn to like yourself! Treat yourself in a positive manner, and show respect for yourself in everything you do. Remember you are not at blame for your job loss, but you are responsible for your job search success. One way to do this is to focus on your

accomplishments. No matter how difficult that may seem, no matter how low you may be or angry or discouraged you are, you have accomplishments! If you didn't, you would not have been hired for your last position.

2. Be positive. Take control and responsibility for your actions, for everything you do. Bad things will happen, but if you own your actions and reactions, you will have a better understanding of your emotions and how to deal with them. Don't take your challenges and struggles personally. It is important to be responsible and learn from experiences and accept them as constructive events or constructive criticism but to remember overall this information is designed to move you in a more positive direction. Use these experiences to grow. Growth is the most important part of the job search process; without growth, you CANNOT be successful in finding new employment or dealing with the job search process.

3. Remember to always grow. Experience from your previous jobs is great, but continuing to update your skills, participating in volunteering activities, and finding a viable mentor or someone to listen and "let things out" are all part of your personal growth process. Achieving this will assist you as each job search situation occurs in your career, whether you are a Boomer, Gen X, or Millennial. By holding onto negative attitude producers, you will produce more negativity. Also plan to take things one day at a time.

Many multi-step programs use this style of dealing with issues that break down the negativity that causes failure so that it can be handled in a more productive and effective manner. Once you start taking things one step at a time or day by day, it allows you to manage negative attitudes and avoid angst. Remember, "Rome wasn't built in a day." Your job search and the emotions that you feel during this time will not be under control overnight, and your job search will not reach final achievement overnight either.

4. Reward yourself. Take time to accomplish something that makes you feel good. Volunteer and keep a list of your successful achievements. You have your OWN permission to see a movie, have a cup of coffee with friends, take a short camping trip, or do some activity that provides positive emotional feelings while you are seeking reemployment. MAKE THESE EVENTS A REWARD FOR EACH TIME YOU ACHIEVE A GOAL THAT HELPS YOU MAINTAIN A POSITIVE ATTITUDE. Over time continued rewards for achieving that positive attitude will become second nature for you, and dealing with all the emotional aspects of the job search will be much more manageable.

STRESS – Stress operates in parallel with attitude and is the "mother" of anxiety.[2] Elizabeth Scott studied stress management and suggests that Reframing is a way of changing the way the job seeker will look at something, thus changing the experience of it. Scott states that by using Reframing, one is able to reduce stress to a minor inconvenience.

Have you had a day when it seems that everything is going wrong until you talk with someone else whose troubles make yours seem pale in comparison? This is one way to recognize that your stressors aren't as bad as you see them in your mind. Even the situation where you may have faced challenges that produced negative and stressful events eventually brought you success and positive results, giving you better control over your stress.

Reframing, according to Elizabeth Scott, is the process that psychologists utilize to help an individual evaluate or examine how they look at the things that produce stress that would affect the job seeker.

To understand the difference between stress, attitude, and anxiety, it is necessary to first return to the definition of stress. ***Stress is a behavioral action that causes a form of fight-or-flight response.*** Usually *stress* is primarily shown in how your physical body reacts to stressors, from how your mind perceives various situations. In many cases, stress and anxiety get confused, and understanding the difference between the two is vital to achieve job search success. According to the National Institute of Health, stress stems from something that makes you feel frustrated, whereas anxiety causes you to feel uneasy, fearful, and withdrawn. Anxiety can be developed by prolonged stressors just from the job search.

Stress is more controlled and controllable than anxiety. Since stress is related to issues, events, situations, and experiences that make the job seeker frustrated, stressors and their physical effects can be decreased and even eliminated, if understood and if time is taken to put each stressor into a compartmentalized action. Simply stated, stressors are decreased and can even go away emotionally and physically by taking this compartmentalizing action, and a feeling of relaxation along with a balance of emotions and physical responses can be achieved.

According to Alex Groberman[3], "an easy way to differentiate the difference between stress and attitude, and stress and anxiety is that stress is a response to everyday pressures. In addition, as previously noted stress is a specific response to a stressor, while in the meantime anxiety may have no definable root cause." Groberman notes that stress goes away as the stressors disappear, but with anxiety and the fact that in many cases there is no direct and easily identifiable root cause, it tends to affect job seekers longer and may need to be treated differently than stress.

There are several actions a job seeker can utilize to manage stress and a short synopsis of this will be discussed here.

As previously noted in this chapter, job loss, unemployment, part-time employment, and underemployment are all issues that can produce stress. At this point it is important to examine the effects stress has on the job seeker in general and point out that they are not simply alleviated when employment is regained. What a job seeker must understand is that the tools and techniques discussed here must be kept in mind and practiced for the next situation requiring a job search.

Losing a job is a stressful situation. This has been repeated multiple times already in this chapter and in the introduction of the book. To many, such as Boomers, Generation X, and even Millennials, it is more than just the way you make a living, pay the bills, and establish socialization with friends, family, acquaintances, and former associates. It's important because of its long-lasting effects and how it informs your actions and behaviors as a job seeker.

As an individual dealing with the stresses of this situation, it is vital that you have the skill sets and abilities to face your emotions when job loss occurs and even when rumors of such things like a downsizing, etc. are first being heard within the workplace. This is accomplished by OWNING your feelings and facing them honestly, and that can be a very scary thought, but it is true! The acknowledgement of your feelings caused by job loss will help you to place those feelings in a proper perspective, allowing you to move forward in the job search. Acknowledge that losing a job is stressful, but also accept the feelings associated with it, put those feelings in perspective, and move forward.

Coping with your job loss and unemploy-

ment. The fear, depression, and anxiety can build to a point that makes it more difficult to get back into the job market. Earlier I noted that job loss is one of the top emotional losses one can feel. It can be as traumatic as losing a loved one. The objective is to accept that there is a process of grief that goes with job loss, understand that process and those feelings, and develop a healthier process to deal with this loss. DON'T be afraid to let your support network see your feelings; that is why you need a support group. You need them to help you get over each step in the grieving process. Remember, like with the loss of a loved one, it is normal to be angry, to be hurt, to feel blame and many other feelings, and they are all normal reactions. Without accomplishing the grieving and coping necessary, your job search time will be greatly extended.

Remember to relieve stress. Reach out to others! This statement brings to light the need to understand what relieving stress is all about. It is rather simple. Letting others know and describing your objectives, not your grief, will offer you as a job seeker emotional control and management for the job search. When you talk to other people, you never know what potential opportunities may arise, what individuals will be willing to offer you all types of support. Even simple expressions of sympathy may give you a "nudge" to reduce some of the stress you feel. Finding ways to talk to others who understand what you are experiencing is vital, required, and helpful to manage stress.

Never forget your family. The most affected people who experience the results of your stress from job loss is your family. Your family can be viewed as friend or foe, and that depends upon how you react or relate to your family by communication and action. Your family can be your most rewarding support network because they know your innermost thoughts and concerns. Do not allow stress to interrupt your family communications and relationships. Tell your family members what is happening to you emotionally, and ask them for things that they think can support you. It is important to accept that your reaction to stress can severely damage family relationships and can cause not only disconnection but also separation of relationships. Remember, any job loss affects the whole family, not just you, and working with your family is crucial for successfully navigating the job search process and the resulting stress.

Learn to care for your health. Slightly different from the previous points mentioned here, it is important that you take action to care for your physical health as well as your mental health. The mind and body work together in dealing with stress. Maintaining a balance in your life will guide you in that aim. Continuing with daily activities, social meetings, and family events are all part of the process of keeping yourself healthy. Remember that change that is not dealt with in a positive manner increases the stressors that affect your thoughts and physical health.

Make time to continue with your daily life activities. The job search is NOT and will never be an 8 AM to 5 PM process. Looking for a job is a job within itself and can even be a seven-days-a-week occupation. Many job search guides written after the Great Recession of 2008 continue to stress that the job seeker must spend "large volumes of time" on the job search. Although this is true, there MUST be a balance between the work of the job search, family, and socialization. In reality the job search, if planned well, can be reduced to four to six hours daily, allowing you to plan for family and socialization time.

Keeping a daily routine helps maintain positive motivation. Routines provide order. Your routines are the time you spend in the job search, outside the home with volunteers, family, friends, acquaintances, and even former work associates. These routines can include having coffee weekly with friends or keeping in good "physical and mental condition" by walking with someone you can talk to.

Dealing with stress boils down to this: Take charge of the things you can control in your life and your job search. You can't control when a prospective employer will call you for that interview. Also, you cannot control the specifics as to how long the job search will take before you succeed or attain a preset goal. You can only control the quality of your job search, so **DON'T WASTE TIME** on those things that are out of your control, out of what you can mold or manipulate in a positive manner. Instead, turn your attention to those things you can control.

Establish a daily, weekly, and even monthly list of those things that will be controllable and aid you in obtaining your objectives.

Realistically, there are almost as many suggestions, methods, and techniques offered by professionals for stress management as there are for developing resumes, cover letters, etc. The next chapter will examine what I believe are the most simple, reliable, successful, and manageable methods. It is almost impossible to fully understand stress and its relationship to your job search until you first understand **ATTITUDE**! A good or positive attitude, a mediocre attitude, and a negative attitude are all phases that job seekers will experience according to their actions during the job search. It is important to learn how to establish, redirect, and remold your mediocre or poor attitude into one that is approaching a positive realm or just being positive while navigating the job search process. In other words, without understanding what attitude is, how it affects your job search, how it defines you in the job search, and how to maintain a positive attitude in a productive way will impact your job hunt success.

Most job seekers start with a positive attitude initially and within a very short period, if the job search begins to draw out, their attitude quickly begins to decline. In my experience, 95% of my clients had already begun to exhibit a less-than-positive attitude regarding the job search and their own abilities within thirty to ninety days of the job search activity. Therefore, learning to understand your attitude and how it affects your job search process will affect your job hunting results. Now it is imperative to determine what is meant by attitude. Attitude is separate from stress and anxiety, but stress and anxiety are resultants of attitude.

2
ATTITUDE: HOW TO DEFINE, BUILD, AND MANAGE IT FOR THE JOB SEARCH

There are millions of Americans that are unemployed, underemployed, working part time, or in contractual work positions. This is the work paradigm for today and, from all that seems to be published about future jobs, the standard for the next decade. This work paradigm began in the early 2000s and manifested itself to the standard for employment in the Great Recession through the present. As many as thirty million and possibly more workers fit into these categories, and that includes those Americans who have stopped looking for work. Many experts believe that these numbers will grow over the next decade. These millions of workers are now suffering from what can actually be described as Post-Traumatic Stress Syndrome, although I doubt there are many psychologists that would agree. This population suffers from increased stress, depression, anxiety, and the physical implications associated with those issues. After the loss of a loved one, the loss of a job has been considered the second greatest producer of stress and anxiety that affects the associated physical health of the job seeker.

The primary point that is being delivered here is that obviously the job search is stressful and can manifest the stress in greater behaviors than "normal" life situations or daily stressors. The longer a job seeker is in the job search process, the greater the intensity that stress and anxiety will have on mental and physical conditions. Stress is not related only your own economic condition, as we see today alone. Instead, stress is related to any time one is in the job search mode.

The primary fact in this statement about stress is that stress relates to your attitude. Attitude is the key to successful job searching. Eli Andur[1], a job career specialist, states that "stress management...is more control than the technical aspects of your job search." Many individuals do not suffer a deficit or lack of ability to develop your personal marketing materials, but according to Andur, "every job seeker suffers from some degree of stress." Many career coaches have written about handling stress or discuss it with their clients, but in general the topic is considered a minor issue. I believe that stress management, anxiety reduction, and a positive attitude accounts for up to sixty percent, or even more in some situations, of your success factor in the job search.

Several associates have asked why go into such detail in this book about where attitude is developed, how to manage it, etc. The answer is quite simple. To understand how you feel as a job

seeker, knowing where those attitudes derive and how to manage them is a must for success. A simple gesture, a statement on a resume, or an error of information on your personal marketing materials are all aspects that can show ATTITUDE IN A NON-POSITIVE WAY and can affect your job-hunting process. There are enough external factors that affect the job hunter's daily life attitude, and the means to ensure a positive attitude in the economic system we face today makes it critical for success. Later in these chapters it will be discussed how to utilize attitude in your job search materials and presentations.

What is attitude?

According to John C. Maxwell[2], "attitude is an inward feeling expressed by outward behavior." Taking the statement one step further, it is how we view ourselves and how others view us based upon our inward feelings and outward actions. Attitude is an action that is expressed by the actions we take during each day's events, tasks, and daily life in general. Sometimes when job seekers are under extreme stress, the "normal" behavior is to cover up or mask our real feelings, i.e. attitude. However, this is at best successful for only a short period of time. Life's early experiences and challenges, we have learned, will eventually fail, breaking down the cover you are using to conceal your real attitude. Eventually, according to Maxwell, attitude manifests itself whether we want it to or not.

A positive attitude is not the only thing a job seeker needs to be successful, but it is the basis for dealing with stress and anxiety in the job search. How each job seeker understands what attitude means and how it is outwardly and inwardly expressed, establishes a methodology to maintain a positive or negative attitude during this stressful experience. Successful events, such as a quick resolution to a job search, will determine how quickly you can regain and maintain a positive attitude. MORE IMPORTANTLY is how your inward and outward attitude is developed and expressed and how it will determine your resolving stressful situations that arise from stressors. Attitude, how to understand, manage it, adapt it, and project it, is a process that must be learned and constantly practiced.

Where does attitude actually play its part in the job search success and the management of stress? First, attitude does not compensate for needed skills, experience, or education. Secondly, attitude cannot automatically manage work, family, friends and relationships. Attitude is the key factor that will allow you to be more successful in managing your job search and relationships. There are positive and negative attitudes, and as individuals we generally change between them multiple times during a twenty-four-hour period. However, it is necessary to learn and to manage the benefits of positive attitude development and the control over our negative attitude and its effects. In addition, it is important to recognize there are many obstacles that will and can affect our attitudes, including disappointments and discouragements, changes in life, work, relationships, and personal finances, fear (of the unknown or unplanned), and of course, failure.

Let's examine how attitude affects you as a job seeker. Attitude, whether positive or negative, is so strong in our daily life that we must be able to recognize them for what they are and their effects upon us.

- *Attitude is the path to developing our job search and job acquisition future.*
- *Attitude tells the world who you currently are, rather than who you want to be; it will affect how employers and employees view the "real you."*
- *Attitude expresses who you were in the past because your past is presented in the current day by attitude.*
- *Psychologists explain that attitude is constantly attempting to express itself in the present, because the past is presented…whether negative or positive.*
- *A positive or negative attitude can be your best friend or worst enemy.*
- *Attitudes will determine how others may or may not want to aid you in your job search.*
- *Attitude is more of an honest view of who you are than your words and sometimes your actions.*

Where do we derive our attitudes? That is the question that job seekers must find an answer to. It is a challenge, in that it must be honest, understandable, and adaptable. Determining where you get your attitude is important, because without that understanding it is impossible to control and manage attitude in the job search.

There are five basic areas in life about how you developed your attitude, according to Dr. Wayne Dyer[3]. Some are easier to understand than others, and some will be more difficult to manage in life than others. Many individuals contend that your attitude is strictly formed by your personality or genetics. Although this is true, it is only one of those five basic areas where you developed your attitude. Here are some summaries of Dr. Dyer's points:

PERSONALITY OR GENETICS Each of you as a job seeker were born with unique character traits, physical features, such as hair color and skin color, emotional responses, etc. In a sense, each job seeker is wired differently, and each job hunter will need to understand that point. Later it will become necessary to understand how to control your personality to establish good and effective relationships with prospective employers, interviewers, friends, acquaintances, networking contacts, and employees you will work with when you regain employment. The point here is for Boomers, X-Gens, and Millennials to remember that you are not forced to act the way you do by your personality and genetics alone!

YOUR ENVIRONMENT AND PERSONAL EXPERIENCES The world around you as a job seeker and your life experiences as you have aged provide you with opportunities to grow and can affect your attitude. Many individual job seekers may or may not carry over these experiences in a positive or negative way from year to year and from situation to situation. Family events such as a parents' divorce, loss of a sibling or spouse, unexpected emergencies all affect your attitude. The most common result is a negative response to negative events and positive responses to positive events. It is important to keep in mind that it always takes more positive events to overcome one negative event. Learning to deal with negative events will give the job seeker a leap over the effects of negativity during the job hunting process.

Personal experiences are not the same nor are they equal for each job seeker. Some individuals have "good luck," some have "mediocre luck," while others just have downright "no luck," in the process. These three expressions are not related to so-called luck alone, but rather to a more scientific analysis of utilizing better skills and ATTITUDE to deal with stress and the job search.

HOW OTHER PEOPLE VIEW YOU VS HOW YOUR ASSOCIATES, PEERS, AND OTHERS VIEW YOU. Do you remember times when an employer spoke off the record but also harshly to you? What about statements by associates that may have hurt you in a job or as a job seeker? Each job seeker reacts differently to hurtful comments, and the less control you have of your attitude, the greater the negative effect hurtful comments will have upon your attitude. Job seekers or employees can overly react to hurtful or negative comments. On the other hand, although negative comments can be hurtful, anyone who has experienced large amounts of negativity may have a more difficult time accepting positive comments and can even within their mind turn those comments into negativity.

Your peers, work associates, acquaintances, friends, and family can also affect your attitude. Psychologists have understood the fact that the more time you spend with people who experience outward negativity, the more you adapt to that mindset; in other words, more positive surroundings, more positive attitude, and more negative surroundings, more negative attitude.

The ability to change or control your attitude from events is not easy. ***If a job seeker associates themselves with individuals who are consistently negative, it will become a dominant behavior, and in a sense, a learned behavior!*** That learned behavior is not complementary to the goals of the job hunter. Hurtful as it may seem, job seekers need to find associates whose attitudes are uplifting and positive to reinforce their own needs. In reality it's all about choices. Surrounding oneself with healthy attitudes is not easy, but it is vital to your job search. It may not change your immediate overall attitude, but it will begin to instill a new positive path of "growth" one step at a time.

Take a look at your environment. You may be negative in your attitude because you don't have the house you want, or the car you want, or the family you hoped for. All that can change, however, by finding and developing a positive attitude in the job search that will spread throughout other aspects of your life. Remember, no one can change your attitude except you. **_You cannot change others nor even the world until you affect change in yourself._**

SELF-IMAGE Self-image, as the father of psychology Sigmund Freud described it, is "the combination of your Id, Ego, and Libido." Without going into psychology, let's just say that self-image is formed and established by multiple parts of experience and attitude. How you as an unemployed person, a part-time employee, or a contractual worker and how you view yourself in the world from that point is your Id. Your self-view of what you can or are achieving in that position or place is your Ego, and your Libido is how you want to perform, your need to perform in the present job or the job you desire. If you view yourself as "the poor employee" not accomplishing a task in a job, or not being able to offer a prospective employer answers to their needs, it will all be present in your self-image, which is shown in your job search activities.

Simply stated, your self-image can represent a poor self-attitude and is reflected in your job search activities that become a major roadblock. Job acquisition specialists, or job seekers, need to use all means possible to eliminate, not build, roadblocks. Most job hunters, especially experienced or less experienced workers, need to take the time to examine themselves in depth to determine what roadblocks they are building and what roadblocks they need to tear down. Managing your attitude will manage the number of roadblocks in your way.

As a job seeker, you must understand where any negativity arises from and how to handle it. Dr. Dwayne Dyer[4] states that "we should examine the labels you apply to yourself. Each label is a boundary or limit you will or will not allow yourself to cross." This is a powerful statement. When you label yourself as x, y, or z, or this or that, it manifests itself in your attitude and also in your actions.

Your self-image is what each job seeker is working hard to improve. Even if you already believe that you maintain and express a positive image, the job hunter must continually monitor the status of your self-image. Your self-image has been developed by multiple factors. Job search success will be controlled positively or negatively by your managed self-image. As I have repeatedly stated in this book, **_you must control your self-image through positive attitude_**. Employers seek qualified and experienced candidates, yet extremely high on their requirement list is a positive attitude in combination with a healthy self-image. A poor self-image will manifest itself at the most critical time during the search process, usually during an interview, and recovering from that image issue is virtually impossible during or after the interview.

BELIEFS - Beliefs can be considered the most important of the five areas where we develop our attitudes. Beliefs can be positive, middle of the road positions, and negative. That is, correct beliefs can be negative either as learned from childhood and experiences or set within your mind from your attitude. As a job search specialist, you must determine what forms and sustains your attitude today, as well as what attitude you want to develop. Your thoughts about everything that touches your life determine your attitude.

Beliefs are initiated in our minds as young children from our parents, playmates, friends, siblings, and extended family. As you graduated from high school, college, and even graduate school, your beliefs continue to develop. Your work experience also becomes part of that learning and development process. Furthermore, as a job seeker, it is integral to your success to separate beliefs between those related to the work acquisition process and everything else that affects your daily life. Author John C. Maxwell's[5] theme behind this idea of attitude is quite to the point. Simply stated, attitude is "the Difference Maker."

What Attitude Cannot Do for You[6]

As I mentioned in the beginning of this chapter, to be successful in the job search you cannot ignore the relevance of attitude to reality and expect to be successful in your job hunt. This means that you are not able to make the necessary changes by only dreaming about changing attitude. Attitude cannot be changed by wishing, hoping, or doing nothing. Action is always required, and practice is necessary in daily life to make changes. The idea that by simply reading a book alone one can change attitude is not a valid assumption. Changing your attitude takes planning and time, practice and more practice, changes in your lifestyle and your reactions to stress in daily life. I'm sure you know or have met many people with great attitudes who have failed to capture their dream, whether it be a job, wealth, health, or a good family relationship.

Attitude cannot make you a millionaire, nor can it alone provide you a new job. However, with the development of a positive attitude, it adds ammunition to your reservoir of skills and other factors to lead you towards you goals and objectives. It is the key factor for your success or failure in life. Attitude is not confidence, nor are the two closely related. Many people think they are the same, but confidence is the function related to skills, experience, knowledge, and abilities. Confidence is generally the feeling that you believe you can do something. What I'm stating here is that although a good attitude can help you personally with your job search, make you more at ease and more pleasant with others, by itself it cannot catapult you into the necessary actions, beliefs, and planning to achieve job acquisition success.

Competence is closer in relationship to attitude because competence supports the development of a good attitude by all the skills you offer an employer. Employers seek competence and a relationship with a strong and positive attitude in today's job market. Remember, jobs today last an average of two and a half years, and your attitude is vital in dealing with this in the job search process.

Attitude cannot replace or substitute for experience either. Experience is the frosting on the cake. As a job hunter, you may have the experience you need for a specific job but need additional updated skills or experience. The difficulty is that you rarely have that added experience until after you need it.

Attitude cannot change who you are and what you have been. Attitude has an impact on your health, mentally as well as physically. Research has shown that people who maintain a positive attitude are more physically active and experience better health than people who maintain a less-than-positive attitude. Certain events or things in your life cannot be changed by attitudes, and this point is important in building a positive attitude.

What does this mean? It's quite simple when you think about it. Attitude cannot change your physical size, such as your height, eye color, shoe size, etc. Some issues related to this can be resolved with other actions, but not with attitude. However, attitude may help you adapt to these challenges much more effectively when your attitude is positive.

Your attitude cannot replace what or how you have grown up. In other words, it takes action to develop what you wanted to be when you grew up. It does not come automatically. This requires action on your part: you must learn what needs to be learned, and you must take decisive actions to become the person you want to be. This is the same for all job seekers. Again, wishing and hoping don't work. Actions are what work and only actions!

To summarize, your attitude cannot by itself make the difference, but it is a great plus. It provides the edge, the framework the job seeker needs to obtain positive results. Learning to understand the components of attitude and how to develop a better attitude requires work, planning, and behavioral changes. It requires commitment, time, and self-honesty. It means having the desire and ability to change your thought patterns, your preconceived ideas and values, and being open to change.

MARKETING - Marketing a positive attitude as a job seeker does not happen automatically. It takes action on your part and that action must be planned and planned again. Most times your initial plan and all the planning work you did has to be revamped to the point that it looks like you are restarting fresh. To many job seekers it may seem like a difficult or impossible task to do the appropriate work to reach it, but with practice, time, and experience, it becomes easier because as one is more focused, the job hunter is more directed to the finished product. Your work to accomplish this becomes an inspired action, and you automatically learn or see where changes are necessary in your marketing planning and actions. These inspired actions, according to some of my clients, are automatic behaviors that maintain a positive attitude by obtaining the ability to eliminate negative ones.

As I just noted, the hardest part about having a good attitude is understanding that it is not something you develop or attain at a split second of time and remains part of you forever. That would be a foolish and misleading notion if nothing else. A positive attitude does not remain in your "space" by itself. There are some methods that can assist you with maintaining a positive attitude:

- When doubt and negative remarks or comments become part of your thoughts or verbal communications, find someone who will tell you

what you are expressing in your communication. Ask these individuals to be honest and make it your commitment to view those responses as positive feedback, not criticism.
- As you may have heard or read a thousand times, find reading or listening materials that will reinforce the changes you are making in your attitude. Keep a monthly calendar and record the approximate time periods where you feel positive or negative in your attitude and note the reasons why. This will give you important feedback for building a more viable internal support system for a positive attitude.
- Find a support group, friend, or mentor who can and will honestly assist you when you are expressing negative attitudes to help you find the reason why that attitude has become prevalent in your mind.

Now that I have discussed what attitude cannot do for you as a job seeker, it is vital to understand what attitude *can* do for you. Attitude can change your whole outlook on the job search. Attitude can take you through any period of negativity you experience, from job application rejections to the next period of job hunting. Attitude is what separates the successful job seeker from the job seeker who is consistently going around in circles attempting to find meaningful employment. Think about who you know as former associates and how they obtained new employment. Are they job seekers who deliberately display negative or mixed attitudes, or are they individuals who have learned to control their outward and inward attitude appearances and mindsets? In addition, what is the key that makes other job seekers attain more networking contacts, interviews, even part-time or contractual employment compared to others? Think about what keeps a job seeker motivated to regain employment, become an entrepreneur, or even write a book on the job search. It's attitude. It's a POSITIVE attitude.

John C. Maxwell[7], in his book "The Difference Maker," states that "most people at the top of their professions are comparable when it comes to talent...the winner's edge is in attitude NOT aptitude. Attitude is the criteria for success." I have had difficulties for many years in establishing my own consistent positive attitude. I suffer from depression and Adult Attention Deficit Disorder, and this has always been an extreme challenge for me. I will admit to you, in many situations I have failed to attain and maintain my own positive attitude. It is something that takes constant work and consistent planning!

My own life crisis brought me to the state of attempted suicide until I learned a very important point about attitude. I learned that most of my clients have or were themselves experiencing depression and that had a great effect upon their attitudes. However, I have learned this and hope to pass this on to every reader. What you experienced in your life, those horrendous experiences and events, affect you based on this one bold point: **YOU TRANSFORM YOURSELF INTO THE WAY YOU WANT TO BE AFFECTED!** Yes, that is correct. When you learn to control attitude, you control the response and effect of negative events and experiences in a positive manner. The more control and understanding of your attitude, the greater ability to cope with any negativity you will come across in not just the job search, but in your everyday life experiences. I do not want you to just accept that each of us can simply take complete control of everything that is negative, but by learning to control your attitude, you respond in more positive ways to negative situations. The more you adapt your attitude, the less effect negative events will have on you and the less self-destruction you will experience.

Here I want to express to you John C. Maxwell's point that the "areas within your control is the difference maker. The greatest difference my attitude can make is within me, not others." Your attitude makes a difference in your job search and life activities. A job seeker's attitude has a profound effect on his or her approach to the job search. I cannot repeat this statement enough times in this book. The happiest people who are dealing with the stresses and anxieties of the job search are those who are consistently attempting to make the best of everything, the good, the bad, and the ugly. Happy people and job seekers who understand their attitude are more capable to deal effectively with challenges that arise.

In the book The Secret[8], one of the basic premises is that life often provides you what you expect from it—what you think about is what you have brought about. If your attitude is negative and you think about not having, you often receive what you ask for!

Your attitude in the job search will affect what you want to achieve and how you will deal with any prospective employers, your networking contacts, family members, friends, associates, and even those individuals you have not yet met.

Your attitude can and will affect relationships with people. To work successfully with people, to obtain an interview, to proceed with each step of the interview process, a job seeker must establish and maintain a positive attitude. A positive attitude provides a way to connect verbally and emotionally with people, especially for the job seeker. President Theodore Roosevelt stated, "the most single ingredient in the formula for success is knowing how to get along with people." Politicians, regardless of their party affiliation, can be good teachers to exhibit how positive attitude affects you as a job seeker. Politicians always present their positive "face" or attitude to the audience, whether they believe it or not. This action provides a connecting point with the audience, establishing attention, listening, understanding and sympathetic alliances. As a job seeker, you must do the same, whether you are in a single face-to-face interview or a telephone interview. It is crucial if you are doing a video interview or sending a video resume to a prospective employer. A positive attitude shows itself in the first minute of a conversation. So this means you must set your attitude mindset before you initiate any conversation.

In John C. Maxwell's[9] book "The Difference Maker," he utilizes four main aspects that are vital to understanding how to develop, use, and maintain a positive attitude. I include this because repetition is one of the most effective ways to learn. Learning is for life, and repetition allows one to reuse and relearn consistently and effectively.

- **"The Lens Principle"**: Who we are determines how we see others. Your attitude as a job seeker establishes the perception of other people. Looking at a prospective employer, the interviewer, a networking associate in a positive attitude, you will more likely view them in a positive manner.
- **"The Pain Principle"**: "Hurting people hurt people and easily hurt themselves." This is a very important and interesting point. As a job seeker, you experience frustration, stress, anxiety, and a host of additional issues. In addition, your past experiences that are not positive will color your perceptions in all aspects of the job search when dealing face-to-face with others. Sometimes it is difficult to understand that you can cause pain to others even when that individual did nothing to initiate such action.
- **"The Elevator Principle"**: This principle has been discussed by psychologists for years. What it describes is quite simple to understand. If you present a positive attitude, you can raise the interest of the interviewer or networking contact. On the other hand, by failing to present the attitude that expresses positivity, the effect on other people can be limited and the results inconclusive or a failure. Job seekers must always establish a positive attitude that makes people want to connect to them and feel good about them.
- **"The Learning Principle"**: Every person we meet has the potential to teach us something. But

most job seekers, who are stressed, angry, and even desperate at times, fail to learn. The stresses of the job search form a cocoon around you, preventing you from learning what you can learn and what others are able to teach you. More people are successful because they have developed a positive attitude that allows them to learn, accept, and adapt from others.

If you are in the job search mode, this last point is important. If you have a track record that is not as good as you would like, it could be because of your attitude. Here I repeat the importance of attitude, attitude, and attitude. Job seekers must be able to develop a positive attitude, regardless of the factors that surround them in day-to-day life. Attaining the ability to be adaptive in your attitude development and with changes and challenges around you will transform them into positive reinforcements in your job search activities and your relationship with those around you. The most important part of being adaptive and maintaining a positive attitude is learning to develop good people skills for communicating and understanding culture and personalities.

In summary, your attitude affects your approach to life and how you face challenges, especially the challenge of finding employment. Have you ever wondered what makes you react to various situations, and how those reactions affect your outcomes and relationships? Developing a positive attitude will not make every resolution to challenges the exact one you desire, but it will provide you with a guiding and positive outlook to develop more meaningful resolutions. In developing more meaningful resolutions to challenges by understanding attitude, the job hunter will be able to manipulate the job search process in a more effective and understanding manner. Understanding attitude allows you to "control" your reactions to your life and the things around it, including the job search. Job seekers who are able to accept the events or situations around them are more adaptable in developing a more effective and less stressful approach when challenges occur.

I urge job seekers to spend time reading about developing a good attitude and positive books, by Maxwell and others. These books will be priceless. The information quoted here and summarized from John Maxwell's *The Difference Maker* will be a game winner, if you follow his simple path.

3

STRESS: HOW TO MANAGE IT IN THE JOB SEARCH

There are probably as many different approaches to this as you see varieties of Campbell's soups in a grocery store. The point is that of all the options available for managing stress, only certain ones will work for each job seeker, so you must find and select the methods that work for you. Some of these options include dealing strictly with the mind or strictly with the body, while others are a combination of both mental and physical activities to manage stress.

There are many different types of stress; however, this chapter will relate to stress from the job search and unemployment. Secondly, it will offer practical options for the job seeker to CONTROL stress. Stress CANNOT be eliminated in the world we live in today, but learning the behavior that will control it and the effects that stress will have on you is important. It does not matter if you are unemployed, working part time, or even working in a full-time position, there is stress, and that stress may be exhibited within you at different levels. However, how you manage stress in your day-to-day activities will allow you to feel better physically as well as mentally.

As you will read in parts of this book, not all stress is bad. "Good stress" can assist an individual with maintaining focus and motivation because that individual has managed time and emotional responses to the stressors. Different types of jobs produce different levels and types of stress. According to the National Institute for Occupational Safety and Health (NIOSH), part of the U. S. Department of Health and Human Services, job stress now more than ever poses a threat to the health of workers and the health of organizations. NIOSH defines job stress as the harmful physical and emotional responses that occur when the requirements of the job do not match the capabilities, resources, or needs of the worker. Stress also occurs when the situation has high demands and the worker has little or no control over it. This also refers to the stressors that affect the job seekers.

What is a Job Search Stressor?

As a job seeker, you should be aware of the **Warning Signs of Job Search Stress**. There are many, but the most common include the following:

- Apathy
- Negativism
- Poor or low morale
- Boredom
- Anxiety
- Frustration
- Fatigue
- Depression
- Self-Alienation from family and others
- Anger
- Physical illnesses

There are two paths that the job seeker must consider when dealing with stress successfully. The first is prevention, or how to keep the stressors from becoming overwhelming stresses. The second is how to effectively manage the new stresses of today's demanding job environment when reemployment is attained. Remember the quote of the former website Careerrealism: "All Jobs are Temporary."

Stress is a normal emotional state. It is actually considered by most health care professionals as the most common issue today within the American workforce. Here are some statistics about stress that provide insight to how it affects the unemployed, as noted by Aneta Peng[1].

- Unemployed and employed job hunters have almost the same level of stress.
- Far more men than women are concerned with loss of self-esteem.
- Job hunters who describe themselves as middle management have the highest levels of stress.
- Stress dramatically increases at the sixth-month mark of unemployment.
- Women are more stressed at the beginning of the job search, while men are the most stressed at the end, i.e. while waiting for an offer.
- 96% of all job seekers managed to reduce or control their stress by using various techniques.

So now you ask, what does this mean to you? It means each job seeker has some level of stress, but the vast majority of stress for job seekers can be managed by learning and using various techniques. It also means that there is nothing wrong with experiencing stress. It is natural, and it is also manageable.

Another successful way of dealing with job search stress is to develop a better way of thinking! That's correct—develop a better way of thinking. One that builds confidence, positive attitude, stress management, and characteristics that present you as the individual that any prospective employer needs.

Do you recognize that each of us have thousands of thoughts taking place in our mind every day? Some studies say we as humans can have as many as 45,000 individual thoughts daily. Understanding how to deal with this deluge of constant thoughts will aid you in reducing stress.

A successful way to deal with stress caused by constant thoughts is to manage a better way of thinking. Many experts believe how we think as well as act will determine our successful approach to stress management. Remember, many individuals have up to 45,000 thoughts per day, and many of these thoughts produce multiple emotional and stressful daily situations. Again, how you think has a significant effect on how you manage stress on a daily basis. According to H. Norman Wright, how we react is far slower.

So the question becomes, are our thoughts harmful or harmless to the job seeker? Thoughts are a chemical reaction within our bodies and those electrochemical reactions trigger a specific behavior. These reactions and associated behaviors set off our emotions. Understanding the emotions and how all these activities function together determine our attitudes, emotions, and behaviors.

According to H. Norman Wright[2], the content of our thoughts matter a lot. Our thoughts can limit what we become. That includes how your job search will be manifested for success or failure. Archibald Hart[3] points out in his book *Habits of the Mind* that your thinking will determine if you will be happy or sad most of the time. In other words, whether you will conduct a positive, emotionally controlled job search or fail to become rehired! Let's review the basis of Hart's proposals.

Self-talk matters in determining whether your job search will be successful or not. Self-talk is simply defined as the thoughts you tell yourself during the job search process, as you move from Step A through Z in finding reemployment. Positive and negative thoughts produce different reactions within your body and therefore how you will react to the necessities of the job search process. ***Simply speaking, we are what we think and what we think determines the success of the job search.***

You Are What You Think

If you are what you think during the job search process, then what does this mean? First, it means that you must redirect your thoughts continually. Two points need to become part of your everyday thinking.

First, when your thoughts are consistently positive, you are in control of your emotions and are able to establish planning that allows you to acquire employment in a successful process.

Secondly, when your thoughts are negative or even toxic, they are controlled by your basic emotions. These basic emotions produce the "chemical" that isn't always reliable. As a job seeker, reliability is vital for success.

Simple psychological processes teach that thoughts, positive or negative, grow stronger together through the process of constant repetition. Take a look around you at others in the job search—do they seem to remain gloomy or depressed for long periods of time, or do they seem to exhibit strong periods of cheerfulness and enthusiasm? Remember that positive thinking like happiness is the result of not just attitude and repetition but also conscious thinking in the "right" way.

Establishing the process for developing positive thoughts needs to be accomplished in an orderly manner and repeated often. This can be done by what I describe above as the process of self-talk! Self-Talk is learning to overcome negative or toxic thoughts and the emotions that are produced from negative thoughts. A job seeker, or anyone who is in a period of stress, can develop positive self-talk strategies by following the processes discussed in this chapter.

Process 1: Mind and Thinking Exercises

This process should be the one you start with each morning of your job search. It is simple and takes no more than five to ten minutes to complete. Archibald Hart calls it the ***"Think Yourself To Control."*** This process kicks the starter on your emotional status before you start your daily work for job seeking.

It is part of the self-talk process. In this process, you simply tell yourself what you are and repeat those statements three times before you start your work. Remember, repetition is the method for how the brain learns. So here is how this exercise works:

On a sheet of paper, list the following items and place a line next to each statement so you can check off that you accomplished that step. The "check-off" action will become a positive reinforcement to assist you in producing a positive mindset. The exercise is designed to build positive thoughts and attitudes before you start your work and reinforce what you set as your objective.

The list can contain the following items:

I am thinking that I am healthy, mentally and physically.	_____
I am thinking that I am successful in what I will accomplish today.	_____
I am thinking that I have no worries or anxiety while I am doing my job search process.	_____
I am not angry, bitter or resentful, that I am seeking new employment or career change.	_____
I am doing my "work" without feeling stressed, anxious, and in control of my emotions.	_____
I am happy today and I will be happy when I finish this work.	_____

Repeat each statement three times, and each time you say it, make sure you say it out loud. We learn and comprehend when we hear more than when we just read a statement. Making a statement out loud reinforces the belief action. Read all the statements three times and place a check for each time you read it on the line. Do this verbal exercise slowly, taking at least fifteen to thirty seconds to speak each statement. Time helps the mind absorb the thoughts you want to remember and act upon. After you have completed the process, begin your work.

I recommend that you repeat this process when you are ready to begin your job search work in the morning, halfway through the process, and especially when you complete the day's plans. The repeated self-talk will reinforce a more positive attitude.

The points to remember from this exercise is that your actions, attitude, emotions are directed by your thoughts, and your thoughts create behavior. As you learn to gain control of your attitude and thoughts, you will also gain control over the challenges of the job search!

Toxic or negative thoughts and emotions are closely linked and can hinder your actions for a successful job search. What happens today is because of your attitude, emotions, and thoughts.

Don't forget that the mind believes negative attitudes caused by stress easier than positive attitudes or emotions. Remember the old statement from Psychology 101: It takes ten positive statements or events to overcome one negative one! It is for this reason that as a job seeker you must build a positive attitude and control your emotions.

Process 2: Analyzing Where the Negative Thoughts Start

This process is designed to assist you as the job seeker in finding where the negative attitudes originate and how to deal with them.

For many people, including job seekers, negative thoughts become a habit, especially as the job search process begins to drag on month after month. During this period, many job seekers begin to establish an addiction to negative thoughts that affect their attitude and increase their stress level.

Author Peter McWilliams wrote in his book *You Can't Afford the Luxury of a Negative Thought* that for many people, negative thinking becomes a habit or even an addiction over time. It is like a disease. He states that not managing negative thoughts and attitude greatly affects the mind, body, and emotions.

The mind becomes addicted to being right, and that does not necessarily mean being positive. As the job seeker becomes "stressed" over the length of the job search process, the negativity becomes the "right" way of thinking, feeling, and even acting. The job seeker begins to accept that failure is the correct attitude and prediction of failure in the job search is the norm.

On the other hand, the body is addicted to the chemicals that are released in the "fight-or- flight" responses, and they may not trigger the positive results you need to acquire to maintain a positive attitude and defeat stress.

Finally, the emotions become addicted to the intensity of all that the mind and body are combating and the intensity of stress continues to increase in magnitude.

According to other experts in stress and depression, naming recurrent thought patterns is a way to help you see your thoughts for what they really are. This is especially important to you as a job seeker because your tasks are more directed at this time to a smaller box of behavior. However, that does not mean your overall thoughts throughout the day do not affect you.

It is important to understand where negative thoughts originate. When you accomplish this, it allows you as the job seeker to gain emotional control over the negative.

Remember, it was noted that as non-positive events occur during the job search, the mind develops a mind tape of thoughts and actions. These thoughts and actions become ingrained in your actions and reactions during the job search process. This exercise will assist you in understanding those negative thoughts and reactions.

I recommend that you repeat this short exercise at least twice a day. Once at the beginning of your daily job search process and at the conclusion of the day's work.

This exercise provides an opportunity to reverse and understand the impact of negative thought patterns and actions. Ask yourself these questions honestly and respond with what first enters you mind. Over time you should notice a change in what is really negative and what is perceived to be negative. Once you begin to notice the difference, your actions will become more realistic and productive.

Process Exercise 2

1. What is the greatest source for your thoughts? _____
   _____
   _____

2. Is there a label you would use to name your most recurring negative <u>thoughts</u> while in the job search mode? _____
   _____

3. What action are you using at this moment to challenge and/or modify those negative thoughts? _____
   _____
   _____
   _____

4. What is the difference between how you think you see yourself negatively vs. how you think you are in reality? (<u>it</u> is suggested that you select only one negative characteristic to reply to at a time.)
   _____
   _____
   _____
   _____
   _____
   _____
   _____

Job seekers present themselves with a negative picture when the job search extends past a time period when employment is expected.

You just read about two processes that aid in developing a positive attitude toward yourself. Doing these exercises repeatedly will retain your positive thought process. It is important to remember that your feelings, attitudes, and emotions are initiated or escalated by what you say and how you react. The more "emotionally" attached you are to an "idea" or "attitude and reaction," the more difficult it is to be objective to the reality of what is real. Repeated self-talk and those exercises will aid in changing your negative attitudes to more positive attitudes. So at this point, the tools and activities provided in this chapter will give you guidance to maintain the necessary attitude for a successful job search.

Now you are ready to answer these questions:

- What evidence is there of these negative or poor characteristics that allow you to present a negative attitude?
- Is there really anything that indicates these characteristics or are they the result of poor self-talk or listening to others around you?
- Would your friends, associates, or others agree with your self-evaluations?
- Are your beliefs or negative characteristics that reinforce your negative attitude accurate after your self-evaluation? If they are, what are you going to do about it? Now, over the next two months, until you regain employment, and for the future?

Earlier in this chapter I briefly discussed self-talk. Let's review what is meant by self-talk before we leave this discussion. Understanding what and how you view yourself as a job seeker is the most crucial aspect of being a job seeker. Attitudes and reactions are derived from your self-talk.

Self-talk is a habit that you form and cultivate over time. If things are going well, much of your self-talk is positive, but if you are having difficulty in the job search, you are building a negative attitude within your mind. Over the years, you have recorded and cultivated hundreds of statements about yourself. The more stressful situations you experience, such as your job search, the more you feed your mind with self-talk.

Each day you automatically pull out of your memory these recorded self-talk statements, and most times they surface unknowingly. You don't initially determine on a conscience level whether it is reality. You don't ask yourself directly, "Is this true?" The more these automatic responses are stated without thought, the less control you have over your beliefs and attitude. Remember, if you fail to thoroughly analyze and determine the "correctness" of your self-talk, your actions and attitude can and most likely will get in the way of reality. As a job seeker, when you spend time on negative thoughts that produce negative attitudes, it can cripple your positive realities and keep you from making progress.

A study showed that "those who ruminated about their problems are four times more likely to develop major depression than those who don't."[4]

Summary on Dealing with Job Search-Related Stress

Many psychologists and specialists on stress have produced dozens of books dealing with stress. The information presented in this book is only a summary of the many common things to do for managing stress.

Although you still may feel that you do not have control over stress, these activities will provide additional assistance during this stressful time:

1. Identify what habits and behaviors are stressors. Look for the real sources of stress aside from what you recognize as stressors. For example:

- Are you explaining stress as only temporary? Temporary stress rarely exists in the job search. It can become an integral part of your daily life. Who are you blaming the cause of stress on?
- I keep a daily, or as daily as possible, journal and write down what stressors I face each day and how am I reacting to them—in a positive or negative way. In addition, I note how I feel after I controlled the stress, so that I can use the same techniques or actions when a similar situation arises.

2. Change your habits of coping with stress into ones that are healthy:

- If you smoke, reduce the smoking.
- Stop taking medication to relax, or check with your doctor first.
- Ensure that you acquire an appropriate amount of sleep daily, and eat a well-balanced diet. Stress can affect you physically and a proper diet will maintain better health.

3. Be active. Exercise of some kind is positive. Doctors have maintained that exercise plays a key role in reducing the physical effects of stress on the body and mind. You don't need to join a health club—you can exercise at home and around your community for free. Some activities to consider:

- Walk each day for at least 15 minutes at a moderate pace, or walk your pet dog for 30 minutes.
- Walk if possible to the grocery store, or other places that you need to visit for personal needs, whenever possible.
- Make this exercising part of your daily schedule and write it down on the daily planner shown earlier in this chapter.

4. Being involved with others is vital to reducing stress levels. Social activities preclude you from constantly worrying and not being productive. Social activities and stress are related in that stress affects specific parts of the body. Social activities reduce hormones that affect the body health and relax the tense feeling produced by stressors. Social activities do not have to be expensive ventures. Here are some that are free or inexpensive:

- Contact former associates, family, or friends for a get-together for coffee or your daily walks.
- Volunteer for an organization that you have an interest in at least once a week. The act of volunteering will distract you from the mental stress and physical issues.

- Take a class for free at a local community college. Most community colleges offer free or nominal charged courses for unemployed people that can assist you with learning new skills to aid in the job search and your skill sets. Online resources, such as Udemy or Coursera, can also help.
- Talk to your pastor, rabbi, or other religious leader who can provide guidance or an open ear for you.
- Write or email friends who you have lost contact with. It may provide you with additional resources that you are not aware of for your job search.

5. Practice controlling your actions and behavior. Although stress is an automated response from your brain and nervous system, some stressors arise from things that YOU can manage. You can handle predictable stressors by changing or modifying the situation in which the stressor exists. Learn to avoid unnecessary stress with these strategies:

- Learn to say no, and know your limits. Stick to your actions so they do not produce renewed stressful situations.
- Express your feelings and don't allow them to be bottled up. If something is bothering you, release it. Discuss it with a person if that is the source, or remove yourself from the situation. Compromise as needed, but only if that action will produce a more relaxed feeling.
- Learn to adapt to situations. Many people during the job search allow the situational stress to prevent

coping mechanisms to function. Deal with issues and management of your time better, and be more assertive.

- Accept the things you can change and learn to let go of those things that you have no control over. In addition, remove those things that are not directly related to you from your mind and actions and "give them back" to the owner of the situation.
- Make time for FUN and RELAXATION. They will do all the beneficial things as noted in this summary. You will feel less stress, manage your stress more effectively, and maintain a better mental and physical state.

4

MANAGING TIME AND CONTROLLING STRESS FACTORS

I know that most older job seekers know the old idiom regarding the Five "P's": Proper Planning Prevents Poor Performance. That has not changed for job seekers today, regardless of their generation, success in the job search, or management of stress and anxiety. Most unsuccessful job seekers fail because, first and foremost, they do not have time management and they exacerbate the effects of stress in their lives and the job search. However, by controlling time for the job search, family, and other necessary events, stress can be controlled and greater positive results are obtained.

Before we get into any processes regarding time management and how it can reduce the effects on the job seeker's stress and anxiety, several points need to be made:

- Developing methods to manage stress and your job

search requires planning, structuring, commitment, and creating a process or system.
- Establishing time management processes that are effective and positive requires some self-examination or introspection.
- Good habits are also necessary, along with good organizational skills, and in most cases these most be developed anew.
- New tools, habits, and skills are also needed to establish a time management system that will assist the job seeker in job acquisition.
- Examining the strengths and tools that you already possess is a key component of this process.

Why is time management such an important issue for dealing with stress as a job seeker? That question is always the first one asked and the most difficult to get a job seeker to understand when dealing with extreme stress.

Time management allows you control: control of yourself, some control of the events and situations around you, and also the opportunity to manage situations based on how they impact you. However, if you do not know your own strengths and weaknesses upfront, you cannot establish a successful time management system that will aid you in managing stress. The more you understand yourself, your strengths, and your weaknesses, the quicker you can establish a meaningful system of time management. This means you must also look for goals that will direct you toward your final objectives.

Most people, as they go through their careers or lives, have a fair amount of knowledge about their strengths and weaknesses. You have worked hard to adapt skills and apply them to your job responsibilities and your personal life. Yet it is a nightmare when you are unemployed and thinking, *What do I do now? When do I do it? How do I do it?*, etc.

When determining your strengths and weaknesses, it is necessary to reaffirm the strengths that will guide you in a positive direction and eventually to control those negative skills that will keep you from moving towards your goal. If you are an individual with ADD or ADHD, it is necessary to take one step at a time and establish written and well-defined methods to keep your time managed.

Time is money, and the time you spend on your job search is going to express the return on your investment for your job search. To manage time, an understanding of the time management process and the one that you will develop for yourself is critical from the start. What is crucial in this exercise is that the most important things are being done first and other things are being done in order of importance. When a job seeker takes the time to assess the value of each task for the job search, family time, etc., then stress is reduced and goals are obtained.

Most job seekers do not understand how to manage time. When are you the most active and alert, are you a day person or a night person, do you get more things accomplished in the afternoon? To establish and manage a viable time management program, you must manage your work time when it is most effective. Each individual works at his or her own pace and needs to understand how that will affect his or her job search.

Dirk Zeller,[1] the author of *Time Management for Dummies, Mini Edition*, notes four points that each person should understand and use to develop an effective time management program:

- How many hours can you work at a high level each day?
- What's your most productive time of the day?
- How many weeks can you work at high intensity without a break?
- How long of a break do you need so you can come back focused and intense?

These are the main questions to keep in mind as you develop an effective time management system to deal with stress and the job search. This will help the job seeker stick to a time scheduling system with the least potential for failure. Developing a time management system requires the establishment of organization. This organization is related to mental as well as physical organizing. It requires a tracking system to record how your time will be spent and how you can manage changes in areas that are necessary.

The greatest cause for failure with a time management system is the inability to overcome time management obstacles. Family and other things can sidetrack your ability to manage your job search process through the time management program you have developed. These obstacles can disrupt your ability to attain the desired goals. There are and will always be interruptions to your time, but how you manage those disruptions will determine how long it will take to find employment and how well you will manage stress.

The number one deterrent to managing a time management system is procrastination. A job seeker must keep procrastination under control at all times. When you fail to accomplish tasks by not following your time management system, you allow stress to creep back into the job search efforts, causing a short circuit of the process.

If that is not enough, another important aspect of time management is the ability to keep yourself in a high motivational state. Dirk Zeller recognizes the use of self-rewards. This can be as simple as taking some time off and doing something that you like for a period of time. The ability to have a positive period of downtime will reinforce your efforts to continue to maintain your time management system.

The first task in establishing a positive attitude in your job search with time management is to prioritize your time. This means it is necessary to set time periods during the day aside for specific actions and things related specifically to your job search. Job seekers who manage and plan, prioritizing their schedule for the day, are more successful than those who don't. What is notable is that job seekers who prioritize their schedule are happier, suffer less down time and depression, and find ways to successfully manage stress.

The only way to be successful is to take several steps first to analyze how you spend your job search time. These include:

- Examine how you spend your time. Not just your time in the job search but each available period of time during the day. What do you spend most of your time doing? Is it working on the job search, doing things that are directly opposite of the job search, or a mixture of many things?
- Determine this by keeping a log of when you are most productive in any activity on your daily schedule. The more times of the day when you are productive can aid you to manage the stress related to the job search because you are focused on a specific task or set of tasks and have the best opportunity and resources to complete those tasks.
- Determine where your interruptions derive from during the day. Are they from the stress you are experiencing and affecting your concentration and energy levels, or are they from family members or other sources? This is crucial for obtaining control of your time planning and the results you need.

Another point of strong consideration and action for the job seeker is to determine goals. Studies have shown that regardless of what the objective of any individual may be, when goals are established the chance for success is more likely to produce the results desired. Remember to keep your goals manageable. That means initially your goals for the job search should be goals that are attainable for each day rather than initially setting goals for a weekly period or monthly period. That can come later because the objective is to establish a pattern of successful accomplishments to relieve stress!

It is necessary to determine what your goals should be, and that is difficult for the job seeker who is stressed in the job acquisition process. In addition, it is necessary to identify how much of your time you spend on each part of your goal process—in other words, how much time you spend in each activity to achieve your goals.

As a job seeker, you can attain this only by asking yourself these questions:

- How much actual time do you spend on job search activities and other non-job-seeking activities?
- What task-oriented or goal-oriented time is spent on other goals or tasks?
- What is the return you are receiving in your job search activities from the time being spent?

To understand all this, it is necessary to establish a simple plan to establish time management so you can reduce stress. Many successful job seekers and successful people already follow this simple and quick process. It is all about prioritizing your time and working with the most important items first, so you feel good about accomplishments.

A simple way of developing time management is to produce a simple worksheet with six columns. Before you do that, write down a list of all the goals you wish to accomplish on a single day relating to the job search. I have three columns labeled A, B, C, with the first letter of the alphabet representing a MUST-DO activity to attain my goal, column B representing the next level down, and C, the least important of all the items in the first two columns. The next column is a statement of what my goal is, job search or some other activity, and the fifth column is the completion date or time that it was completed. The last column is the actual work that needs to be accomplished toward achieving a daily

goal. This will later be matched up with a longer term sheet that I use to manage goals with realistic time expectations.

101 State Street
Albany, New York 12308
555-555-1212

James McCarthy,
Sr. V.P. Human Resources
Capital Development Corporation
8812 Union Street
Albany, New York 12308

August 12, 2020

Dear Mr. McCarthy,

I am a successful business professional with a proven track record of growth and restructuring of mid-sized corporations. I would bring my penchant and experience for success to your organization in the capacity of a senior executive, for which my skills are well noted.

- A strong commitment to the industry, having contributed my talents in the commercial construction industry in various roles and responsibilities.

- Solid marketing and fiscal management background to implement, understand, and troubleshoot various operations in the organization.

- Throughout my experience, I have maintained an entrepreneurial philosophy along with the knowledge and willingness to be adaptive that will bridge the multi-sectors of an organization such as yours.

- Over the last ten years of my career, I have demonstrated forward thinking and strategic initiatives that transcend the current state of the organization to deliver profitability and achieve growth, needed in the tightening economy of commercial construction this decade.

I have earned an MBA degree in Strategic Business Development and have held multiple leadership positions in my career. My education and experiences further bolster my qualifications and abilities to complete the job required.

I would like to discuss with you the experience and value I will bring to your company as I have done so often in the past.

Thank you for your consideration.

Sincerely,
James Smith

In the job search there are short-term goals and tasks each day, weekly goals and tasks, and tasks that are longer in nature. By combining both forms with what is to be accomplished daily and relate that to the time periods broken down on the Goal Form, the job hunter has the opportunity to visualize realistic accomplishments that are measurable and positive. Positive reinforcements reduce the negativity of stress.

101 State Street
Albany, New York 12308
555-555-1212

James McCarthy,
Sr. V.P. Human Resources
Capital Development Corporation
8812 Union Street
Albany, New York 12308

August 12, 2020

Dear Mr. McCarthy,

I am a highly skilled business project manager with 10 years of a professional proven track record of growth and restructuring of mid-sized corporations. I would bring my experience for success to your organization in the capacity of experience working with firms similar to those you work with. I would make an excellent and productive addition to your team.

My work in project management has afforded me advanced knowledge in developing scopes and keeping projects on time and budget. Moreover, my years of experience have provided strong experience for all parties involved in commercial construction. In addition, my previous position afforded me a well-rounded skill set, including relationship building and tie management skills, which are exemplary.

- Outlining project scopes and modifications, managing timelines and deadlines.

- Consistent and accurate reporting on overall progress.

- Managing daily operations and implementation of new programs and changes.

- Forecasting project revenue and ensuring all goals are met to specs and on time.

In addition to my experience and relationship building, I have a solid educational foundation and a desire for furthering projects that build loyalty and, in turn, grow revenue for the organization. I would appreciate the opportunity to contribute to your ongoing growth and continued success.

Please review my attached resume for additional details regarding my experience. Do not hesitate to reach out if you have any questions for this open position. I would love to meet with you to discuss this position in more detail.

Thank you for your consideration.

Sincerely,
James Smith

People fail to achieve goals because they don't plan the process thoroughly. It is necessary to establish daily goals that are achievable, providing you with positive feelings and work side-by-side with longer term goals that take more than one day to accomplish. That is why I developed the Goal Form. I achieve more success and reduce stress when I can measure day-to-day accomplishments and relate them to the actual time it may take to obtain a specific goal. Although this chapter is centered around utilizing time management for the job search, it is important to understand that while you are in the job acquisition process, your entire life and its activities are affected. Let's look at this a little closer.

There is a third form that I use to manage my time each day and that includes a daily time planner. I place the most important items that must be completed that day in my calendar and those that are level B then level C in importance. This provides you with two daily references to achieving your goals daily and a long-term attainment form to measure your achievement.

When you use the daily time planner, you are not only able to provide greater success opportunities for your job search, but you will be able to plan other events and activities along with family time. However, the critical point is that you will have visual reinforcements to keep you focused and reduce stress on a day-to-day level.

As you put your daily to-do's on a daily time calendar by time, you assure yourself the appropriate time is mapped out to complete that task, whether it is job search related, dinner out with the family, or any other activity. Maintaining a flow of work that is focused is important to achieve the job search goal, keep a balance with family, and manage stress and the anxiety stress produces. Each day review your tasks or to-do list with the tasks completed, evaluate if more time is needed for similar tasks, and adjust your schedule as needed. You should see improved results each week if you follow a system such as the one just outlined.

DATE	TIME	
	7:00	
	7:30	
	8:00	
	8:30	
	9:00	
	9:30	
	10:00	
	10:30	
	11:00	
	11:30	
	12:00	
	12:30	
	1:00	
	1:30	
	2:00	
	2:30	
	3:00	
	3:30	
	4:00	
	4:30	
	5:00	
	5:30	
	6:00	
	Evening	

The most important aspect of time management success is controlling the factors that distract the focus you need to be successful. Controlling interruptions such as telephone calls, kids knocking on the door, and many other things is your task. You need to limit interruptions and determine whether anything that does distract you from your focus is an immediate need or something that can and should be put off later until you have completed your tasks. Once focus is taken away from a task, it can be extremely difficult to regain that level of activity or even complete the objective for that day. Block off time periods on your daily time schedule to return calls. Prospective employers do not expect you to be home just because they are calling you. Allow them to leave a voice message or even a text and answer it when you have it planned as part of your daily work schedule.

Finally, the number one killer of accomplishing a task for the job seeker is procrastination. When you feel stressed, you lose your focus and will want to do anything that gives you immediate distraction from that stress. Once procrastination is present, focus, motivation, attitude, and task fulfillment is difficult to regain or achieve. Remember:

- Procrastination reduces the time you have to actually achieve a task in your job search. Your net results are generally not up-to-par with your abilities, and that is how you will represent yourself in the search.
- Nothing goes away because you put it off until later. Most job seekers who put off the necessary planned

actions usually increase stress levels and anxiety. Stress becomes an overriding factor when you go back to the task.

According to Dirk Zeller,[2] there is also "good procrastination." Although this sounds contrary to what I just stated, it is also important to understand in managing job search stress.

When is procrastination acceptable?

- When you are pressured to accomplish a task and are forced to make choices that may not be the ones you need. You are not clear headed enough to focus on the conditions around you to successfully complete the task. Think about how many times you prepared a cover letter or modified a resume at the last minute and then regretted information included or misspellings in the documents after you sent them.
- When the time is not right to attempt to focus on a task, there may be too many interruptions or stimuli going on around you, keeping you from doing the best you can in accomplishing that task.
- Finally, have you ever had a time when you had several things that had to be done at the same time, as most job seekers have? The understanding is that taking a break or procrastinating for a short period will provide you a greater insight as to which things are more critical than others and aids you in

returning to a high-activity level and staying focused.

Tracking time will assist in how you manage the activity included in that time period will be an aid to assist in managing stress. Time management is an excellent process for developing the focus needed in your job search, and recording what stress you are experiencing and how you are handling it will benefit your success. Unless you know what stressors are producing the stressful situation, there are no methods that can adequately reduce it or aid in developing a positive focus toward achieving your job search goal.

As part of a process that I developed for stress management, I have added one additional component. That component is meant to assist you in managing not only your daily stress vs. goals, your short- and long-term goals and daily stress factors, but in evaluating your stress management related to those goals. This is accomplished by keeping a record of how stress is evaluated and your plans for managing the stressors and allows feedback as to your success or need for a redirected approach.

Today is _____	Stressor	How Am I Handling This	Managed	
			Yes	No

Now that you have read about stress and how to utilize another approach in managing it through time management, understanding and dealing with the stressors should be more organized and less frustrating.

Mary Eileen Williams[3] specifies a specific way to control stress by managing progress and making the actions you take tangible. She states that most people spend a lot of time expending a lot of energy without seeing a return on those efforts. In her article, she promotes the necessity and value to recognize the investment of time and efforts that are spent. The activity of using a checklist and other materials to track your success provides the job seeker with that return on investment that is visible and measurable. Utilizing a tracking system gives you a sense of making progress. Recognizing that your planning results in progress toward your job acquisition goal reinforces the continuous process of developing and maintaining a positive attitude.

Williams also notes that it is necessary to give time to "tender loving care." By developing a workable time management program that promotes progress and tangible results, those results will certainly seem easier to attain. This includes getting proper rest and sleep, exercise, and some small rewards on a regular basis.

Finally, Nathan Newberger[4] reviews strategies for managing stress through time management skills and a time management system that have been written about in many job search manuals. These suggestions by Newberger are a continuation of what many job search professionals have promoted for decades. Here are some of Newberger's examples of what to do:

- Keep organized. When you are organized, you are not stressed when you need to find something or must complete an urgent and unexpected task.
- Maintain a schedule and keep to it. As a job seeker, you need to recognize that the job search is like having a full-time job. If you are just "busy" without a schedule or goal plan, tasks produce stress.
- Take time for life. As a job seeker working full time, it is important to take time for YOU! Take a break to prevent the buildup of stressors that keep you from being focused. Keeping a schedule will afford you the time to take a break that is needed and time to add some fun into your life.
- Understand where you are heading. Stress is created by you. As a job hunter, you can create stress by not evaluating or measuring where you stand or are heading in your employment process. Take time to review where you need more assistance in the job search. This means tasks like how your correspondence with a prospective employer has been received and how effective other forms of communications have been in producing results for you. Review the impressions you have made in interviews and your development and utilization of networking contacts.
- Keep away from repetitive stress. Your work on managing stress will improve your efficiency of

stress management. Practice will assist you in the efficiency in dealing with stress management. Efficiency does not mean taking shortcuts by using repetitive job search marketing materials, but rather the ability to adapt existing material to different situations and opportunities without stress.

Another well known expert in the job search is Dr. Richard Bayer,[5] who offers similar suggestions to Mary Ellen Williams. Dr. Bayer offers several suggestions which are noted briefly as they have been repeated by most professionals in the job search field:

- Realize it's okay to be between jobs.
- Stay in touch with your former colleagues and friends.
- Treat your job search as a full-time job.
- Exercise regularly and keep a healthy lifestyle.
- Enjoy the change of pace.
- Stay away from negative news and naysayers.
- Don't be afraid to vent!
- Look at unemployment as a business problem and handle it as such.
- Celebrate short-term successes.
- Keep on top of your skills and knowledge.
- AND HAVE SOME FUN!

5

EFFECTIVE COMMUNICATION IN THE JOB SEARCH

Every time you speak, utilize body language, or state an opinion, there is an opportunity to evoke stressors, giving rise to stress. If you have had multiple interviews, networking contact opportunities, and face-to-face meetings that did not present the results you desired, stressors arise, causing a loss of focus and the necessity to manage stress yet again! When the phone fails to ring, or you do not receive an email requesting a desire to meet to discuss a possible opportunity, old negative habits push you to the point of stress where control is potentially misdirected or lost. Communication is a learned process from practice and self-examination. Whether the communication is via a cover letter, resume, email, telephone or texting, or face-to-face dialogue, all that you say and how you say it will determine the success of your communication and the message you are attempting to present. When you fail to communicate in a manner that does not connect with the individuals in your arena, you are unable to successfully present your message and the individuals will be unable to receive that message correctly. This can also lead to added stress.

Communication is a two-part process, sending and receiving, and job seekers like yourself will fall into two groups. The first are those who have trouble talking to others and presenting their message, and the second are those who have trouble listening. How you talk and how you listen will determine your level of job search success. Speaking and listening effectively are skills that are learned by practice and experience. In the fast-paced world of today's job seeker, these skills must be up to date, and a job hunter must constantly understand the jargon used in conversation despite generational gaps. Millennials use terms and expressions differently than Gen Xers, and Boomers generally communicate in a style more formal than Millennials. Understanding what is expressed across this generation gap will assist the job seeker in their job search.

A job seeker cannot fake genuineness. What does that mean? Simply, you cannot fake interest in communicating with another individual. Body language will give you away each and every time. It is easier to get positive communication by speaking honestly and expressing interest in the conversation or communication with others. Dale Carnegie stated, "you can make more friends in two months by becoming genuinely interested in other people than you can in two years by trying to get other people interested in you." As job seekers, your key is to connect via communication with a prospective employer through the interview that you are interested in their company, their company's needs, and the opportunity to solve their needs, rather than attempting to initiate a conversation where you are the center of attention.

All this can only be achieved by confidence, and confidence is established when stress is managed and processes for communicating confidently are understood. Since every individual you interview with will have a personality that is different from yours, it is vital to find multiple ways or styles that make communicating effective and successful. Stress will be eliminated when you as the job seeker can appreciate the ability to communicate effectively with an interviewer or networking contact, especially with someone you have just met.

It is important to remember again that learning to communicate in the job search process will not happen overnight, regardless of how successful you think you are. You are the worst judge of your own skills here, and will obtain success when you have communicated the information you wish without expressing or emotionally questioning what you have achieved. Changes in how to communicate is accomplished in small bites and through practice. Your speaking techniques, how you present your "perceptions," and learning to focus on the conversation should always be checked and focused upon as part of your learning process. When you manage these factors, you will be able to achieve stress management successfully. Successful communication, as I noted, takes practice, finding commonalities, learning to focus, listening and speaking skills, and preparing what you want to communicate. When you understand these processes and steps, then you can successfully communicate with confidence.

Effective communication takes practice and preparation. I repeat this again because it is vital for successful and effective communication. Communicating requires the need to find commonalities between the speaker and listener, as well as the ability to develop the listening and speaking skills mentioned above. It is not difficult to find a starting place because all job seekers use talking and listening skills all the time. What is needed is to learn the process of how to focus on these skills to improve what is said and the ability to understand what is being communicated by the other person. Most interviews fail because the job candidate fails to understand what the interviewer wants, and the interviewee fails to communicate what needs to be communicated. This will continue to produce stress in the job search if the job seeker cannot accomplish this task.

Communicating effectively can reduce some levels of stress due to the fact that proper focus is on the appropriate techniques. It would be a false analysis if I stated that there will be no stress producers if you learn the appropriate skill sets for communication. Many other factors will play into the arena, challenging you to constantly modify your focus and how you speak and listen during conversations. This is still common for individuals who are at the peak of their careers, as well as new job seekers entering the market for the first time.

Many of my clients have asked me, "How do I know if I have issues related to stress in my job search?" It is amazing that many job hunters have never established any planning for how to communicate effectively and thus are left with this situation. Many job seekers are so out of touch with themselves that they are unable to place into words the physical symptoms of stress that are affecting them. So to make it easier for the job seeker, entry level, middle level, executive level, professional level, white collar, blue collar, or any level, here are some symptoms that tell you when you are having a stressful situation in your job search:

- *Sweaty palms of your hands, either constant or intermittent, before, during, and after a discussion or interview.*
- *You perspire more than usual.*
- *You have that acidic funny feeling in your chest.*
- *Your tongue and mouth are dry before, during, and even after the interview or meeting.*
- *You forget what you want to say or ask, or even how to appropriately answer a question.*
- *Your mind goes blank.*
- *Your feet tingle, and your hands or even your toes and the bottoms of your feet are cold and/or damp.*

- *You start to have muscle cramps or need to use the restroom even though you just used it!*
- *You stutter in your speech, your voice trembles, or your pitch raises in comparison to your normal voice.*
- *Your hands shake for no reason that you can imagine, and you may even begin to tap your foot on the floor.*
- *You think about ways to cancel the interview appointment or networking opportunity.*

Okay, relax, let's have a little levity and slow down. These symptoms are common in any high-pressure environment, such as a telephone interview, an online interview over Skype, the initial face to-face interview, or the multiple interview process after you pass the initial interview. These symptoms are normal according to many specialists in human behavior, who may downplay them. I've had clients who believe that these are their personal "job marketing portfolios" that are announcing their nervousness, their lack of skills and experience, and the question "why hire me?" to a prospective employer.

Mike Bechtle,[1] author of the bestselling book *How to Communicate with Confidence*, presents several methods to manage stress in communication and conversation. He refers to his process as "channeling stress." No matter how hard you may try to appear controlled in each job search situation, these symptoms will appear as stress in one form or another. Bechtle states that sometimes job seekers will feel they are a personal business card announcing their nervousness to anyone they are meeting. Unfortunately, these are challenges that must be overcome. The greater the challenge, from an interview with a single individual to a panel stress interview situation, the more stress will be produced and the more it will need to be controlled.

Earlier in this chapter, I related several characteristics of stress to you, but Mike Bechtle introduces additional stressor situations that many job seekers do not consider. According to Bechtle, you get stressed mostly in social situations:

- You are afraid you will end up alone with no one to talk to—at a networking event, for instance.
- You as a job seeker will run out of things to say.
- In an effort to be adaptable to a conversation, you want to be clever but your inner thoughts make you aware that past experiences mark you as boring.
- As a job seeker, you are afraid and therefore stressed about the overall impression you make, which is a combination of several stressors from my list.
- You are afraid of saying the wrong thing and being embarrassed or more seriously losing the opportunity to receive a job offer.

See how many additional situations in your own life that are stressors that can or have hindered you from initiating, maintaining, and concluding positive and result-oriented successes? Although an earlier chapter discussed managing stress through time management, that process does not always produce effective results by itself. In the rest of this chapter, I will discuss Overcoming Barriers to Communication, Finding Common Ground, Starting and Continuing an Effective and Positive Conversation, and Successfully Ending a Conversation.

Overcoming Barriers to Communication

In a perfect world, you would start a conversation speaking and the other person would simply listen and understand what you are saying. Then you would reverse roles and the process would continue until the parties are finished. You would both understand one another and the message would be clear. How many times have you viewed your conversations that way? Unfortunately in the real world, it just does not work that way.

We think that conversations will work the way we want without any effort or thought to the possible barriers to communicating. The problem arises when the speaker and listener do not give the same meaning to the words that are spoken. When we speak, we use filters that can and do affect the actual meaning to what you as a job seeker are attempting to get across. What are these barriers?

- Language. Do you speak English and the other person French, for example?

- Background/Socioeconomic Status. Is one speaker from a high economic background and the other from a lower economic background with different experiences? Or is one person is from France and the other from England, with different cultures and experiences?
- Education. Education provides the speaker and listener with higher levels of vocabulary that another person may or may not understand.
- Culture. Individual cultures present different mores and values that may not be common to each party in a conversation.

Words may seem normal to one party but not to the other. The filters are the way each party in a conversation interprets the information presented and that filter can affect how the job seeker is viewed during the interview or networking event. Filters, such as those noted above, affect and determine what we do, what we feel, and how we interpret what we hear. Unless each party understands the way filters can affect commonalities, they can produce barriers to getting the desired results. Success, according to Mike Bechtle,[2] depends on whether or not the filters we have produce barriers. According to Bechtle, the only way to be in conversation is to focus our efforts on being ourselves. You cannot make another person like you, but if you can be genuine, it gives the other party in the conversation a chance to respond to the real you. This does not mean you are a "bad" person. It means that the person chose to respond that way, and how that person responds is out of your control. Remember the more you attempt to control the other party in the conversation, the more the other individual will become frustrated. Again, remember that conversations are two-way streets and no one, especially a job seeker, cannot control how the other individual will actually respond in a conversation. Most of all, there are no guarantees that all conversations will be effective and comfortable. It is not necessarily true that you can assume responsibility for failure. It takes two or more people to have a conversation and it takes everyone involved to make it successful.

Finding Common Ground

Common ground means finding mechanisms that both parties in a conversation understand. That could be the same language, background, acquaintances, associates, employer, or others. Everyone shares something in common, and it might take a while to find it, but if used appropriately a conversation can produce successful results.

How do you as a job seeker find a common ground to produce effective results? The answer is not as complicated as one might think. The answer was already stated earlier in this chapter: to stop thinking about what you bring to the conversation and start thinking about what the other party brings. Utilize the knowledge and experience of the other person to gain perspective and develop commonalities in your conversation. It is not easy to find that common ground. The key is to explore what commonalities you and the other party might have. Finding commonalities allows you to talk about more things. It allows you as the job seeker to expand the number of topics that are available in your discussion. Using a different perspective allows you to see a broader picture of the other person in the conversation.

Bechtle notes, when you only look through your own perspective, you wonder how you are coming across to the other person. When you as a job seeker are in a conversation, listen to the words of the other person, watch their expressions and gestures, hear the tone of their voice, and don't make assumptions about what is being said. Placing yourself into the perspective of the other person in a conversation helps to eliminate false assumptions.

When barriers are broken down, it allows you and the other party to contribute to the conversation. As a job seeker, you may have a limited amount of information to contribute, but looking through the perspective of the other person opens the conversation opportunities and will make the conversation more effective. It also:

- Takes the pressure off. You no longer have the pressure of measuring how you come across to the other person in the interview.
- Removes the guesswork in the conversation relationship.
- Eliminates false assumptions in believing that the other party has the same opinion and interests as you.

Starting and Continuing an Effective and Positive Conversation

For many job seekers the task of starting a conversation that is effective and positive is a difficult venture. Why is it so difficult for some job seekers to initiate a conversation? The answers are individual personality types, stress levels, and preparedness.

- Many job seekers don't know how to initiate the conversation, and this is where a conversation is doomed from the start. They fail to take the time to map out first on paper prior to the planned conversation the objectives or practice what they want to accomplish and how to achieve it.
- Even when job seekers have "some idea in their mind" about what they may want to say first, second, and third, it might not be relevant to what is necessary for this type of conversation. Here the problem relates to the first point of failing to plan ahead.
- Many job seekers who attempt to enter into a conversation fear that what they want to express to another individual might not be relevant or that they will not know how to express that relevancy. Planning is the only thing that will provide the job seeker with success in this situation. Many job seekers do not know what to say first or second or

how to overcome the stress of initiating a conversation.
- They question whether the other person in the conversation even wants to have a dialogue with them, or the other person selects other conversation topics they did not plan for. Are they able to keep the conversation on relevant topics without fear of losing direction in the conversation?
- Stress produces for a job seeker a tendency to want to rush into a conversation without verbal and body language signals that are part of the acceptance that it is alright to start your conversation. When this part of conversation, in networking situations for example, is not planned and practiced in advance, stress builds and everything you want to accomplish is unsuccessful.

For the job seeker who is more introverted than extroverted, these can be the doom of your whole conversation experience. All the points listed above are the questions that you must ask yourself prior to initiating any networking conversation, conversation related to discussing employment opportunities with others, and conversations with associates once employed. Successfully overcoming these obstacles will provide you with greater success not only in your job search occupation, but for your success in your new employment opportunity and when a job search event reoccurs.

To take this one step further, many job seekers in networking situations and in general conversation have a tendency to prejudge before they complete the first step of the conversation. The job seeker, who allows stress to override his or her plans for a conversation, will have the negative result of mentally perceiving that the other person will not be open to the questions of topics to discuss. The initiator of the conversation will fail to develop common groundwork to begin a successful conversation due to poor stress management.

Do not attempt to "read" the body language or verbal signals with a preconceived negative mental attitude. Instead, mentally plan a positive action that because you have successfully planned your communication with this person, you will cross successfully any body language or verbal signals that will cause your message to be deflected. Failure to accurately interpret the verbal and body language signals of the other individual in the conversation will produce negative results. Remember this, and I cannot emphasis this enough, that every negative action has far more negative results than a positive action. A job seeker who is unable to understand the required communication process with another person may and usually will force that other person to pass along his experience with you to other individuals. As a job seeker, you cannot afford to have this in your networking contacts, interviewing opportunities, or any other conversational experience you may have related to your job search AND with your future employer.

This is such an important topic that I want to take a step back and reiterate some of these very important points pertaining to successful conversations:

- If you maintain an assumption that you may be intruding into a zone that is personally uncomfortable without prior preparation, the most likely result will be failure of having a successful conversation. Networking is just one form of conversation this happens with, more so than in a face-to-face interview situation, but is also quite evident in telephone interviews!
- Remember that interviews, especially networking interviews, require structure to initiate and continue the conversation. You as the job seeker are the individual who MUST be responsible for maintaining that structure in the complete process.
- On the other hand, DO NOT expect that you will fail to develop a successful conversation with someone. Regardless of how much planning you have done, there may be an individual with whom you cannot establish the needed "chemistry" for a conversation. This is no different than asking someone for a date, and not being able to advance to a second date because there were not enough similarities. The point is that you planned your approach and you did not allow a negative result to deter you from your planned OBJECTIVE!

I have seen too many job seekers fail to obtain successful conversation for networking events, interviewing opportunities, and loss employment opportunities due to the fact that they have failed to understand, accept, and utilize good communication practices. Success takes planning and practice, and there is no way to get around this point. Just as you examine the culture of a prospective employer, you must examine your plans for developing a successful and meaningful dialogue with another individual or group of individuals while you are in the job search.

Finally, I have seen many clients who fail at communication during networking opportunities or initial interviews because they assume the other person in the conversation is more confident than they are. Developing confidence is a work in progress, from making a plan, working that plan, determining your stressors and how to manage those stressors, building confidence with positive feedback during your conversations, and continually balancing all these processes at the same time!

Remember this and you will have more success:

- Accept the fact that many people act as though they are highly confident but only have learned the ability to express confidence as you must do. They may be as nervous and stressed during the conversation in a networking situation or an interview. This is managing your stress using what you have learned.
- Many people, according to Mike Bechle, [3] "may stand aside or alone from others, in a social function, because they are waiting for someone to approach them [...] In addition, many feel a lack of confidence

because there is a doubt regarding what the other person may like to talk about." This can all be overcome by utilizing the tools for managing stress and developing the tools and techniques for a successful conversation that you have learned and practiced.

Once a conversation is initiated, the objective is to maintain it until you reach the expected results. You MAY NOT reach or obtain all the results you expect, but you will attain results to assist you in your job search process. You will have succeeded in establishing successful common ground and have the other party's attention. Then you will notice how your efforts of preparation have begun to work for you. As you continue with these successful experiences, you will feel empowered and your ability to have similar experiences will grow.

Successfully Ending a Conversation

You have succeeded and completed a conversation, whether it be networking, an informational interview, or just talking with other job seekers. So now what? You believe you have the answers to your questions and that they have been received, evaluated, and stored for future use. Or have they?

Introverts and extroverts can make the inevitable false assumption that just because a conversation seems to have concluded, the conversation was a success. In many cases, just the opposite is the truth. A large percentage of conversations end due to the fact that the initiating party has failed in one of the following ways.

False assumptions are made that the "real purpose" and "objectives" of the conversation were met. In fact, many job seekers forget the total objectives or become confused and disorganized because of stress. In this situation, the conversation ends abruptly and unsuccessfully. You must maintain in your mind the outline of what you want to achieve in the conversation, so that when it is time to conclude, you have met the real objectives.

This activity takes practice, as noted earlier in this chapter. There is nothing erroneous in preparing 3 x 5 cards in advance with your questions and objectives ahead of time, so you can review them and practice them in advance and refer to those notes during a conversation. If you receive a queried stare from the individual you are speaking with, explain that you are reviewing why you asked the person to speak with you. Over time, you will have this ability mentally stamped into your behavior pattern and may not need to pull out any notes on a card. Time is money, talk is a value to the one you want to have a conversation with, and being prepared is the key to success.

As Mike Bechtle[4] notes, conversations end in two ways: a satisfying conclusion or a painful escape. In a successful conversation, the skills expressed in this chapter will leave all parties with a positive feeling and allow for future discussion with the same individual or others. Mental preparation of how to have a conversation eliminates the conclusion that your encounter was a waste of time and reduces the reinforcement of stressful situations.

To point out again, conversations must proceed with a design from initiating to conversing and finally to concluding. However, oftentimes instead of concluding a conversation, you stay too long, and your questions become boring, repetitive, and off topic. The conversation drags, and there becomes an effort on your part to keep it going rather than measuring the success you achieved to that point.

End the conversation when your objectives are met or met to the best of your abilities. Don't push the other person into a position that becomes uncomfortable and risks the opportunity for further discussions. Some methods to concluding a conversation include:

- Finding and/or establishing prior to the discussion when you will terminate the dialogue.
- Reinforce the key points that were discussed in a way to express appreciation to the other individual.
- Always share some key information back to the person who has provided you with their time. Sharing information, in turn, reinforces a desire to continue further contact and discussions.
- Don't forget to say thank you, leave a business card if you have one, or send a note via email or hard copy expressing your appreciation.
- At the first opportunity, put down on paper what

information you gleaned from the conversation and you can utilize it during your job search.
- Ask the other individual if there is any additional assistance you can provide, and then depart with a polite gesture and thank you.

6

DEVELOPING A POSITIVE MARKETING
PORTFOLIO FOR YOUR JOB SEARCH

Everything you do today in the job search represents your attitude. A positive attitude expresses the value you represent to potential employers, and a negative attitude expresses a lack of self confidence in yourself. As the job search process changes constantly, you as a job seeker must maintain your personal "selling/marketing" materials in a positive way.

During the last five to ten years, a new term has been used that covers the resume, cover letter, references, work examples, recognitions, awards, and anything else related to your career success and employment. This new term is called ***Personal Job Search Marketing Portfolio***. Although this term may not be as common as it was, it does refer to your total job search presentation materials. Just as the work paradigm has changed, the way you as a job seeker sells yourself has changed and will continue to change over the next decade.

Many of my clients ask the same questions: Are resumes outdated? What type of resume should I use? Do I need to have a cover letter in the age of digital job searches? Will the job search paradigm continue to change? Well, the answer is Yes, Yes, Yes and always Yes! Strategies will change constantly, but the processes will remain constant. The only constant is that there is no constant. Technology will continue to play an increasingly important role in the job search.

In this chapter, you will learn how to develop a successful and positive Personal Job Search Marketing Portfolio. As a job seeker, you will learn how to develop the positive cover letter, resume, effective **"Why Hire Me"** letter, and other materials to sell yourself to an employer. In the job search, employment, and interviewing realities of today, just preparing a resume and sending off a cover letter with it is no longer sufficient. Employers want to know more before you meet first on the screening telephone interview or the first face-to-face interview.

The materials you present in your Personal Job Search Marketing Portfolio will continually change! Just as work has a new paradigm, so will the requirements on how to sell yourself to an employer. How you present yourself to a prospective employer will telecast your positive or negative view of yourself to the individual who reads your information. As a job seeker, you want to always present the best picture of who you are: your experience, your skills, your achievements, your desires, and especially how you will fit into an organization.

How do you accomplish this task? That is the most difficult aspect of selling yourself. Each part of the job search process will be part of your Personal Job Search Marketing Portfolio. These include the following:

1. Targeted cover letter that matches you directly with the requirements of the job.
2. A "formulated" resume that highlights your successful experience related directly to the prospective employer.
3. A "Why you should hire me" statement.
4. A form that adequately spells out successful achievements you have made in your past jobs.
5. And yes, even a printed letter with the references **YOU WANT** the prospective employer to contact to support your selling efforts.
6. All this is to be bound in a clean and presentable folder and presented to the hiring manager after the interview process. In many cases, you may need several of these during each interview.

This book highlights the need for a positive attitude and job searching materials, but much of what you need is already presented in books such as *Resumes for Dummies*, 7th edition by Laura DeCarlo, founder of the global organization Career Directors International and Certified Master Resume Writer.

Laura DeCarlo[1] notes that at some point in your job search, you will want to inform a prospective employer why you are the correct candidate for a position. The resume must tell the employer in a straightforward manner why:

- You are the best match for a specific job.
- Your value will matter.
- Your skills and specific experience are essential to the bottom line.
- You're worth the money you hope to earn.
- You're qualified to solve the employer's problem.
- Your accomplishment claims can be believed and are related to how you will add value as an asset to the employer.

Trends for Now and Beyond

Every year the trends for developing the tools for your job search go from minor to major changes in thoughts, actions, and development. There were significant changes in the development of job search tools in 2015, and those changes seem to remain constant for the next few years.

Some clients have asked: Why worry about changes? Will employers actually notice the changes in the presentation, production, and utilization of the job search tools? Aren't most employers using some type of computerized program to check for keywords, key experience, and key requirements? Well, the answer is yes to all those questions. Although all employers do not employ the use of computerized software, they do establish their own criteria for getting to the first interview and past the "gatekeeper."

Who determines what criteria is appropriate for developing how you produce your Personal Presentation Materials for employers? In reality, that is not an easy question to answer. Sometimes employers will delineate what type of presentations are acceptable, and other times it will be the career industry that emphasizes what methods are appropriate for job seekers. Regardless of the source, the materials must represent your positive attitude.

Resume Trends for Now and Maybe Tomorrow

Many experts have written about the trends for proper cover letters and resume writing for 2019 – 2021. As jobs become more competitive and challenging, so do the tools you need for your presentation. The average job still takes a minimum of six months to acquire and as a job seeker, plan on another month for each $10,000 in earnings after the $50,000 dollar income level. There have always been and always will be multiple thoughts as to what will be considered appropriate trends from one year to another. I always recommend to my clients to review the trends and use what is most professional, eye catching yet non-flamboyant, clean, organized, and shows you to be the best candidate for the position.

These trends in jobs don't change dramatically from year to year, but you will need to learn new techniques and methodologies. What does change are the following areas:

- **Technology**
- **Skill Trends**
- **Economic realities and available jobs in the market**

You as a job seeker cannot do much about available jobs and the economic conditions, but you must be able to deal with changes in technology and what skill trends are demanded for the job market. By being prepared, you will maintain a positive attitude in your search and the results will be more productive. However, knowing the general health of the economy and how your specific industry is faring will aid you in the job hunt. That knowledge may also be necessary in determining whether other changes, such as a move away from a specific industry, are warranted.

1. An important consideration for this year and beyond is the resurgence of understanding and promoting "soft skills" along with your "hard skills."[2] According to 77 percent of employers surveyed, soft skills are equally as important as hard skills. These percentages have not changed significantly over the last five years. Here are the ten most popular soft skills employers say they look for when hiring:

- **73% Work Ethic**
- **73% Dependability**
- **72% Positive Attitude**

- **66% Self-Motivation**
- **60% Team Orientation**
- **57% Multitasking**
- **57% Works well under pressure**
- **56% Good Communication**
- **51% Flexibility**
- **46% Confidence**

However, saying that you have a "Positive Attitude," for instance, is not good enough; you have to show it. Provide an example of how you present a positive attitude in your job and how it reflected on your team or other work associates, and of course your own performance. A hiring manager will question you on these soft skills as much as the hard skills of technology and job skill sets.

2. Shorter is better, for this year and beyond. Keep your information short and concise. Do not list information that is not relevant to the job you are seeking, or that may raise questions related to your ability to do the job.

3. Fads in resumes and cover letters are unpredictable for results. Not all fads will create the impression you intend.

Functional resumes focus primarily on your skills and accomplishments and may not provide context necessary to your work experience. There is still a skepticism regarding this approach due to the fact that some hiring and HR people feel the candidate is hiding something such as a gap in employment. It is vital to use this type of resume or video resume in specific ways—either if requested or if the demand for the job requires more emphasis on skills and achievements over actual job history. Employers like resumes with appealing and simple formats. Customize your resume format to optimize your qualifications and experience.

4. **Appropriate white space and less condensed but precise verbiage is better.**

Too much white space or overcrowding on your resume or cover letter will make a reader go directly to the next applicant.

5. **Templates are gone!**

Generic, pre-built resume and cover letter patterns, formats, and adaptable templates are for the past. Since the year 2008 and onward begins the year of the individual. **HR Managers and Hiring Managers want to see a candidate for "real." They want to see how unique you are as a job candidate.** All this by using a plain resume format.

6. **Remove unnecessary components of the resume and cover letter.**

Objective statements are for the past. Instead, simply state the position you seek and support it with rest of the document.

There are four trends for **Cover Letters in 2020-2021**. Although some of these may seem small in certain ways, they are in reality very important. Louise Kursmark,[3] author of multiple sources of job search books, relates four specific trends for today that have carried over from the last few years. Job seekers need to modernize their job search cover letters. The simpler and more concise, the more appealing to the reader. Concise cover letters, though, are not resumes.

The four trends that Kursmark discusses are:

Trend 1: Cover Letters Become Shorter.

At the time a prospective employer reads your cover letter, he or she knows nothing about you. After a cover letter is read, the reader is deciding to place you in the keep pile, reject pile, or maybe that dreaded trash pile. The more difficult a letter is to read, the less positive results you will have. Don't cram your cover letter with unnecessary information.

I inform my clients to make their cover letter so interesting that the reader will want to know more about them. As a matter of fact the reader MUST know more about you! Do this in a positive written set of statements that are direct and

precise, and pertain to the value you WILL add to the company.

Cover letters should be limited to no more than one page. Each paragraph should be no longer than three or four sentences—less if possible. Your letter should be easy to skim for facts and should be easy to read on paper or a computer screen.

Trend 2: Cover Letters Add Value to Online Applications (and MORE!)

When an application indicates that a cover letter is optional, you should always include one! When employers scan the numerous resumes to choose which slate of candidates to interview, the information presented in the resumes begins to look similar. Everyone applying for the specific position is attempting to match the qualifications necessary. When you include a cover letter, you can share specific additional information that highlights you.

This additional information is specific to you and your skill sets and achievements that will stand out from the pack! Here you can employ and emphasize specific aspects of your background, such as hard and soft skills that fit particularly well. By accomplishing that, you can form a connection that will identify you with that specific job and company. Remember, the objective is to set you apart from other candidates.

. . .

Trend 3: Cover Letters Digital Notes

When was the last time you actually mailed a cover letter and resume to a prospective employer? Very few employers ask you to mail a cover letter or resume today. In today's job market, the answer is that you will probably never send a resume or cover letter again, unless the online digital application asks you to cut and paste or attach one.

Laura Kursmark refers to cover letters as E-Notes. When you are not uploading your letters to an online application, you are sending them via email. That means your letters should be formatted as e-notes (an email message) and not a traditional letter.

An E-Note contains:

- No letterhead at the top of the page.
- No non-informative sentence announcing that you are applying for a particular position. That should be listed as the subject of the email.

Trend 4: Good Writing and Correct Spelling and Grammar Never Go Out of Style

Your cover letter is a less formal e-note or uploaded file. It is written to the point and dispenses with unnecessary courtesies that you may have used in the past, but in poor taste!

However, that does not mean you can dispense with utilizing correct spelling and grammar.

Employers judge candidates on the quality of the documents they submit in a job application. Remember, these are a reflection of the quality of work you will do for that employer if hired.

Take the time to read and reread for proper spelling and grammar. Then take another time to reread for content to assure that you are presenting the information that will make you stand out above other candidates.

Producing a Positive Attitude Cover Letter

What is meant by producing a positive attitude cover letter? Simply that, as a job seeker, you do not compose any negative statements in your short space allocated to get the reader to want more!

Follow these general guidelines:

- Do not include statements that you are seeking better opportunities.
- Do not say your position was eliminated or you were eliminated.
- Include a specific statement that explains how you meet the requirements of the position.
- Ask for a meeting by the factual information you

provide in the cover letter.
- Exclude falsehoods or exaggerations in your information.
- Grammar and spelling are correct.
- Follow the trends for cover letters to the best of your ability.

By following these tasks and developing an informative cover letter, you build and support your positive attitude. Remember that there are hundreds of candidates applying for the same position you seek.

In the job search process, the cover letter still plays a vital role, a much more expanded role than it did just a few years ago. Cover letters can be an introduction, a mini combination of the standard cover letter with targeted highlights from your resume, and even a targeted presentation to an employer.

In the job search of 2020-2021, there are two types of cover letters. The first is what I refer to as the standard introduction-position seeking style and the second is the targeted cover letter. I believe we mentioned this, BUT HERE IS A REMINDER!

The standard introduction-position seeking style cover letter is where you, as the job seeker, are asking an employer if there are any present or upcoming position openings. You do not have any information that confirms this employer has any openings, but you have the skills and background necessary to fill a specific set of positions, should there be an availability. As a job changer, this style of cover letter would fit into your planning process to develop your personalized job search marketing tools.

The second style of cover letter is the targeted style. This cover letter is more direct when you are informed by a source that there is a specific job opportunity with an employer. You design your cover letter to target the specific job and requirements in your cover letter to meet what is necessary for consideration.

Sample Non-Targeted Cover Letter

                                                                                            101 State Street
                                                                                            Albany, New York 12308
                                                                                            555-555-1212

James McCarthy,
Sr. V.P. Human Resources
Capital Development Corporation
8812 Union Street
Albany, New York 12308

August 12, 2020

Dear Mr. McCarthy,

I am a successful business professional with a proven track record of growth and restructuring of mid-sized corporations. I would bring my penchant and experience for success to your organization in the capacity of a senior executive, for which my skills are well noted.

- A strong commitment to the industry, having contributed my talents in the commercial construction industry in various roles and responsibilities.

- Solid marketing and fiscal management background to implement, understand, and troubleshoot various operations in the organization.

- Throughout my experience, I have maintained an entrepreneurial philosophy along with the knowledge and willingness to be adaptive that will bridge the multi-sectors of an organization such as yours.

- Over the last ten years of my career, I have demonstrated forward thinking and strategic initiatives that transcend the current state of the organization to deliver profitability and achieve growth, needed in the tightening economy of commercial construction this decade.

I have earned an MBA degree in Strategic Business Development and have held multiple leadership positions in my career. My education and experiences further bolster my qualifications and abilities to complete the job required.

I would like to discuss with you the experience and value I will bring to your company as I have done so often in the past.

Thank you for your consideration.

Sincerely,
James Smith

Sample Targeted Cover Letter

101 State Street
Albany, New York 12308
555-555-1212

James McCarthy,
Sr. V.P. Human Resources
Capital Development Corporation
8812 Union Street
Albany, New York 12308

August 12, 2020

Dear Mr. McCarthy,

I am a highly skilled business project manager with 10 years of a professional proven track record of growth and restructuring of mid-sized corporations. I would bring my experience for success to your organization in the capacity of experience working with firms similar to those you work with. I would make an excellent and productive addition to your team.

My work in project management has afforded me advanced knowledge in developing scopes and keeping projects on time and budget. Moreover, my years of experience have provided strong experience for all parties involved in commercial construction. In addition, my previous position afforded me a well-rounded skill set, including relationship building and tie management skills, which are exemplary.

- Outlining project scopes and modifications, managing timelines and deadlines.

- Consistent and accurate reporting on overall progress.

- Managing daily operations and implementation of new programs and changes.

- Forecasting project revenue and ensuring all goals are met to specs and on time.

In addition to my experience and relationship building, I have a solid educational foundation and a desire for furthering projects that build loyalty and, in turn, grow revenue for the organization. I would appreciate the opportunity to contribute to your ongoing growth and continued success.

Please review my attached resume for additional details regarding my experience. Do not hesitate to reach out if you have any questions for this open position. I would love to meet with you to discuss this position in more detail.

Thank you for your consideration.

Sincerely,
James Smith

The Resume

The first thing I recommend is that you stop using the old resumes that you have lying around your home office. They are or will be ineffective in today's ever-growing competitive and challenging job market. Generalizations of a job candidate's work history, accomplishments, and recognition will no longer suffice by themselves.

Secondly, there are dozens of books that have been produced on writing the "correct resume style" for your job search. ***In this chapter, I will discuss what I believe to be the best "generalized" approach for developing a resume that reflects a positive attitude***. I recommend you read several other books on the full dynamics of resume writing that have been published within the last few years. Remember trends change and books published prior to 2015 may not be up to date on resume trends. Let's get started with developing your positive resume as part of your personal job search marketing portfolio.

The **"Targeted Resume"** is still the newest, most successful style in the resume tool box. Just as the plain cover letter and standard resume was your "Bible" for the job search for the past couple decades or longer. Resumes, chronological, functional, and hybrid, have been annotated to hiring trends, especially over the last several years. As the job market continues to become more and more complicated, each step of the process requires stronger and more in depth navigational paths. As stated above, the old generic style resume is no longer the "golden key" to the tools for the job seeker. Where the generic resume was designed to show your core competencies and abilities for a job in the demanding job market of today and the foreseeable future, the targeted resume is designed for the specific job for which you have the best skills, most qualified experience, transferable skills, and diversity to be successful.

In the targeted resume, you as the job seeker address the following major points:

- ***Clearly express your qualifications and why you are the best match for the job.***
- ***Use powerful words and statements to persuade and attract the interest of the employer.***
- ***Express and highlight your strengths and downplay points that may undermine your attempt to acquire an interview.***

In today's employer job market, it is many times more important to utilize targeted resumes. Without this consideration, it is almost impossible to get your resume to the hiring manager.

Remember generic resumes are passé. A generic resume does not express your values, your positive attitude, or your specific experiences and accomplishments as related to a specific job position. Simply, generic resumes lack the motivation and key aspect of informing an employer who you are and what you can do for that employer. Again, generic resumes show a lack of positive attitude!

It is imperative to know the difference between these common or general resumes and the value of the targeted resume.[4]

Common/Generic Resume	Targeted Resume
One size fits all	Customized to fit
All purpose	Tailored to fit
"A CORE" style	Personalized
All in one	Job specific

Ask yourself what style puts you in the best light to a prospective employer. Choosing the appropriate style or format of resume will determine how you appear to an employer and will assist you in demonstrating a positive attitude. Remember, there are at least a hundred resumes submitted for every job opening, according to recruiters, and now even more so in 2020.

Why does a customized or targeted approach work more effectively?

- Employers are still inundated with hundreds of resumes for a single position. Imagine if a key decision maker was responsible for filling more than one position—how little time would be relegated to reviewing each resume?

- A targeted resume places keywords and descriptions related to the position up front and center. Automated software is designed to seek out these key words and elements for the position and also note where they are lacking. An A-T-S resume scoring system places a score based on keywords and other factors on each resume examined via this system. The higher the score related to the number of key words and phrases found by the software, the greater your chances that your targeted resume will be considered.

If you have a generic resume, here are some key steps to modify it to a targeted resume:

- *Read the job description to determine exactly what the employer seeks for the specific type of position. Are you really interested in the position? List on paper the key words and phrases used in the job description and make sure that those same words are used in your resume and cover letter. Remove anything that does not apply to the position requirements.*
- *Remove all irrelevant context from every section of your resume that does not apply to the job requirements and may distract the reader from viewing your qualifications and experience. Too much*

information can make you appear overqualified or underqualified for the position. Assure that your skills are relevant and up to date for the skills required for the position.
- *A resume should speak directly to the position. Use terminology in the context of the specific job, as well as language utilized within the industry related to the position.*
- *All key words and phrases you need can be found within the body of the job posting, whether it is online, print, or word of mouth. Your skill listing must include the key skill words that connect with the responsibilities in your professional experience section of the resume. Do not include keywords relating to skills and experience if they do not exist within your work history.*

Developing A Resume That Will be Effective

There are two major considerations when developing what a job seeker should include within a resume. First is to consider that technology has grown over the last decade and will likely be utilized to a greater extent in evaluating your resume before any "human" resource individual may read the resume. More and more corporations, non-profit organizations, and smaller companies are utilizing or rely upon "A-T-S Friendly" computer software. ***The purpose of this software is to scan YOU OUT OF QUALIFYING for the position.*** A-T-S computer software is used to scan your resume to search out keywords and "your specific" experience, plus your honesty!

A job seeker who presents an honest resume will maintain the positive attitude necessary for success over one who worries constantly about the false information that may be inserted into a resume.

A-T-S software is intuitive and continues to be developed as a source of artificial intelligence for resume reviews. It is now also being used to scan cover letters. Its main purpose is to seek out the best candidate and qualify one job seeker over another. So now, more than ever, you always want to show your best side.

It is also important to discuss the resume format or style that a job candidate should use. Consider and use these rules as guidelines:

1. *<u>Format matters!</u> All employers do not use the same software in reading resumes, written or e-documents. For the vast majority of resumes that are submitted for review, best practice is to submit the resume in .txt or plain text format. If a*

prospective employer directs you to send a Word document, .doc, .docx, PDF, or some other type, it is for a reason. The primary reason is ease of reading the document, either by a human or software. Otherwise text format, .txt, is the best selection. This document format can be easily opened and also maintains its design characteristics with other document software. It is clean and can easily be read by the gate-keeper, HR, or the hiring manager.

2. *Plain text format, .txt, should be used when an application requires the candidate to cut and paste a resume into a dialog box for an e-document. Word documents and other types may not be easily readable when printed, although there has been improvement in the software. Word documents especially are likely to not show as clear and clean in some document software or various versions of software. Avoid headaches and being dropped from consideration because your resume in unreadable.*

Robyn Schlinger,[5] who is considered a pioneer in the development of the ATS formatted resume, recommends the following for an "A-T-S Friendly" resume's specific context and style:

- If you are not a good match for the job, don't attempt to trick the system. (A-T-S software is constantly developing, and it will discover your actual fitness for a position quickly.)
- Apply only for the position for which you are qualified and include all relevant information for the position.
- Include all necessary key words and phrases found in the job description. Remember these are part of the scoring.
- Emphasize any technology listed in the job description.
- Modify your resume for each job to match what the employer is seeking.
- Keep your formatting simple. Fancy characters, graphics and tables can hurt your resume.
- Ensure your resume is readable by humans and computers. Read your resume over for spelling and grammatical errors.
- Use your word processing software to produce your resume. The most common is the Microsoft program Word. Save your resume in .txt, doc, or docx format for easy reading.

A-T-S resume programs are designed to read set formats. The more non-conforming the format of a resume, the less information is decoded. Your resume in general should follow this layout:

- **Contact Information**
- **Summary (to include only the name of the position for which you are applying)**
- **Professional Experience. In this section of the resume, be sure to use formal titles for each position you held. Include responsibilities and measurable accomplishments with key words and phrases as related to the position and your experiences. Repeat keywords from position to position in your resume to score higher with A-T-S software. Also show increased levels or experience and responsibility.**
- **Education. Place the full name of the school/university/college, location, and degree or certification earned. Do not include GPA or year of graduation.**
- **Training. Record your relevant training that will aid in the selection process only.**
- **Certifications.**
- **Skills. Describe skills with words that newer versions of A-T-S software consider keywords.**

When you don't have a specific required skill as noted for a position, make reference to the fact that you are capable of learning or performing a specifically required skill. Also, if you are knowledgeable about a particular skill or software program, be sure to state that.

Resume Example 1 – A-T-S Resume Format – Chronological Format[6]

Jennifer Richman

City, State Zip
(206) 555-5555 • jrichman@email.com
linkedin.com/in/your-name-here

WORK EXPERIENCE

Company 3, Location
Job Title ___(MM/YYYY)-Present

This is where you write about your experience. Do not simply list your day-to-day job duties. Work in resume keywords that are most relevant to the job for which you're applying. Try replacing some of your duties with measurable results and accomplishments rather than duties. Remember, "duties tell, accomplishments sell." To create a strong measurable result, try this format: [Action verb] [brief explanation of accomplishment] resulting in [quantifiable outcome. Using %, $, etc. will draw the eye and make an impact]. For example: "Responded to an average of 203 customer service emails per week, improving response time by 74% and customer satisfaction by 31% between 2016 to 2017."

Company 2, Location
Job Title ___(MM/YYYY)-(MM/YYYY)

Keep your sentences short and to the point. This will make it easier for a recruiter or hiring manager to read or skim. Use your limited space to focus on things that are most relevant to the new job, rather than going into every detail about the responsibilities that took up most of your time. Tailor your resume to the job description.

Company 1, Location
Job Title ___(MM/YYYY)-(MM/YYYY)

It's OK to leave positions off your resume if they aren't relevant to the job you're pursuing. Unless the experience is crucial, you can also go into fewer details on older positions.

EDUCATION

Degree, (Do not include date of graduation)
College Name, Location

Resume Example 2 – A-T-S Resume Format – Functional Format[7]

Tamara A. Jefferson
City, State Zip | (206) 555-5555 | TamaraJeffersson@email.com | linkedin.com/in/your-name-here

CAREER SUMMARY

Add a resume summary that highlights what it is you do, the types of companies you've worked with, and why you're great at your job. Typically summaries should be very short and to the point, but you can go a little long in the functional resume format. Consider including experience levels, specializations, or areas of interest. Ensure that your summary perfectly aligns with what is asked for in the job description.

SKILLS AND STRENGTHS

- **Skill 1** - List your most relevant hard skills, soft skills, and experience for this job.
- **Skill 2** - Mention the skill then briefly add some context to it.
- **Skill 3** - For example (hard skills):
- **Forklift Operation** - OSHA certified forklift operator with 5+ years of experience and a perfect safety record
- **Skill 5** - Another example (soft skills):
- **Multi-tasking:** Met visual design deadlines on overlapping projects in fast-paced agency environment; used project management apps like Basecamp and Trello to keep organized.

PROFESSIONAL ACCOMPLISHMENTS

- Example: [Action verb] [brief explanation of accomplishment] resulting in [quantifiable outcome. Using %, $, etc. will draw the eye and make an impact]
- The best resume accomplishments measure your results in terms of dollars, percentages, or time-saved. Use numbers whenever possible.
- Accomplishment 3
- Accomplishment 4

WORK HISTORY
Company 3, Location, Job Title, (MM/YYYY)-Present
Company 2, Location, Job Title, (MM/YYYY)-(MM/YYYY)
Company 1, Location, Job Title, (MM/YYYY)-(MM/YYYY)

EDUCATION
Degree, Graduation Year (do not enter graduation date), College Name, Location

Resume Example 3 – A-T-S Resume Format – Hybrid Format[8]

Marcus O'Brian

City, State Zip | (206) 555-5555 | mobrian@email.com
linkedin.com/in/your-name-here

Add a strong resume summary here that highlights what it is you do, the types of companies you've worked with, and why you're great at your job. Include experience, specializations, areas of interest, etc.

SKILLS AND ACCOMPLISHMENTS

- SKILL TOPIC 1 (e.g.: Software Engineering or Project Management): Skill 1 | Skill 2 | Skill 3 …
- SKILL TOPIC 2: Skill 1 | Skill 2 | Skill 3 | Skill 4 | Skill 5…
- ACCOMPLISHMENT 1: [Action verb] [brief explanation of accomplishment] resulting in [quantifiable outcome. Using %, $, etc. will draw the eye and make an impact]
- ACCOMPLISHMENT 2: …

WORK EXPERIENCE

JOB TITLE | Company 3, Location (MM/YYYY) – (Present)

Because you listed skills and accomplishments above using this hybrid format, you can afford to write a little bit less in your experience section. Expand to two pages if necessary, but keeping your resume to one page is a good goal to have (unless you have over 10-15 years of relevant experience).

JOB TITLE | Company 2, Location (MM/YYYY) – (MM/YYYY)

It's OK to leave positions off your resume if they aren't relevant to the job you're pursuing. Unless the experience is crucial, you can also go into fewer details on older positions.

EDUCATION

DEGREE | College Name, Location

Other points to remember for e-forms used in job applications:

- An e-form such as a job application completed online in most cases does not represent a legal document or any legal status when you e-sign the application. However, in many cases your cover letter and resume will not be reviewed without the completed form.
- Follow the directions associated with the digital form. Cut and paste as requested or directed and answer all required questions. An incomplete form will usually disqualify your resume from being reviewed.
- Check and review all spelling and grammar before you submit any digital document. Digital forms may not be able to detect spelling or grammatical issues, but should your resume be passed forward to a hiring manager, you may be disqualified. Remember it may pass the ATS software scan, but it will most likely fail the human test, and good HR personnel and a hiring manager will notice such errors.

As a final word about e-documents, A-T-S software may have the final say as to whether your resume will be reviewed by a human. **Online screening software replaces the secretary as the doorkeeper or gateway to the hiring manager.** Therefore, you must follow the requirements to succeed to the next step in the interview process.

Online screening or prescreening, whether it is A-T-S or some other type, is an automated process of creating a memory that will analyze and store requirements for a job opening. It then collects, collates, and matches the information submitted by each candidate. This ATS software is designed to assure and verify that you have the requirements necessary, that you are who you say you are in your resume, and that your background information is truthful. A "no" or "incorrect" answer to specific questions on a digital document can automatically disqualify you from consideration.

Review - Here are some areas that online screening will filter:

- **Whether the material presented in your submitted resume a direct copy of other scanned resumes.**
- **The same information on cover letters.**
- **Specific abilities and skills that require pre-training or experience for a skill.**

Review - Selecting Your Resume Style (Format)

Everything that will happen in the job process and your activity as a job seeker revolves around how a prospective employer views you! Are you positive in your attitude, or negative? Does your attitude show, does stress show, and how do you express it in a document? Are you a good candidate who is a good fit for the position? How do you best exhibit your skills, abilities, and other qualifications, and match those to a job that you seek? All this is presented in your resume.

Resume formats do matter, and employers have their own beliefs regarding which resume represents the real you and whether you are an honest and most qualified, or non-qualified candidate. A job seeker should examine if a job posting lists a desired or required format of resume and secondly review the information requested in the job posting. This can include:

- List increasing responsibilities in each position on your resume.
- Describe your analytical skills in each position, based upon each specific situation you faced in a job.
- List all positions you held in your work career.

Remember as I close this chapter, this book is dealing with managing stress in easy and proven ways. It has been written for you as a guide to manage your emotional battles during the job search. These are simple techniques that have been successful for many job seekers and I hope for you.

There are many excellent books on cover letters, resumes, interviewing, networking and other aspects of the job search, and many of those authors have been referenced in these chapters. Allow this book to be an emotional guide for you while in the job acquisition process along with others.

7

POSITIVE TOOLS, METHODS, AND TECHNIQUES FOR A PRODUCTIVE AND POSITIVE INTERVIEW EXPERIENCE

How many times have you sat in front of an interviewer with sweaty palms, a damp collar, and sweat in the armpits? I am going to teach you how not to sweat about it and how to manage the interview stress. As a job seeker, you can handle the stress by completing a simple set of exercises and understanding what is taking place during the interview process. The largest percentage of job seekers have the greatest period of stress during interviews, and that is due to a lack of understanding of yourself and the interview process. The interview process is not meant to be friendly! It is designed to "weed out" any potential candidate who is non-qualified. However, most candidates forget that you are being interviewed because you are qualified, and you just need to believe it and act upon it. Why else would you be sitting in front of an interviewer or online for an interview?

The primary objective of any interview is to present yourself in a positive manner. As a job seeker, it is vital to understand the job interview process and the psychological processes that are taking place. **Remember I stated that the interview is a "weeding out process."** You need to change the direction to one in which you are planting the seeds! The initial interview, whether on the phone or face to face, is like plowing a field for the year's harvest. Taking the process one step at a time will provide you confidence, strength, and success under virtually all interview situations. ***This chapter will briefly touch on the six main type of interview situations you will face and how to emotionally prepare to handle each one successfully and maintain a positive attitude throughout the entire interview process. This chapter will deal primarily with how to manage stress and your behavior during these interview formats.***

Mind Confidence Exercise & Reminder

Do you know this statement?: "Whatever the mind can conceive and believe, it can achieve." This statement of self-belief is attributed to Napoleon Hill and Clement Stone, two well known, positive motivational authors, speakers, and trainers as well as advocates for positive mental attitudes and success. This belief statement is the basis for a short exercise I developed for my clients prior to entering into any interview situation. This exercise will provide you balance and a positive attitude, regardless of what questions or style of interview you face as a job seeker. Practice this exercise the evening before your interview and one hour before the scheduled meeting interview time. In fact, I recommend you write it down on a 3" x 5" or 4" x 6" card and place it in your note pad or tablet, in your notes on your smart phone, or anywhere you can refer to it prior to your interview. ***These affirmation statements in this example will cement a positive attitude of reinforcement.***

The exercise is one designed to train the mind to develop new self-beliefs. Clement Stone, insurance magnate and philanthropist, knew the value of self-belief and was instrumental in developing the phrase "Whatever the mind can conceive, it can believe." This same statement is relevant for you as a job seeker. Repetition has always been considered a part of "internal mind learning," and this exercise is just one small part of that.

Upon completing this exercise, close your eyes and take several deep breaths. Picture within you mind's eye that you are calm, relaxed, in a location that makes you feel at ease, and even surrounded by whatever adds to that feeling. After that review, in your inner mind, ask yourself what are the reasons THAT YOU ARE BEING HIRED for the job you desire? Imagine that you have already achieved that goal and are at the new job starting the first day. Remember your self-talk is your strength. Repeating this simple repetitive exercise will provide you confidence for any style of interview you will face.

"Whatever the mind can conceive, it can achieve"

CLEMENT STONE

Step 1.

I am who I am, the best that I am, and I follow the path of strength and my abilities: My strengths include:

Step 2.

This interview is not a judgement of me personally, it is a measurement ONLY of what I have to offer the employer. It is also a lesson of what additional training I may require. My strengths include:

Step 3.

I am strong in skills, passionate, experienced, knowledgeable of tasks required, and reflect positively when I represent myself to others. My strengths include:

Step 4.

I am not judged as an individual, only in my skills that I bring to the job, my experience in previous work, knowledge I possess, and HOW TO USE THAT KNOWLEDGE for this new job. It is NOT an evaluation of who I am, only what I can and will provide an employer. My strengths include:

Step 5.

My mind can conceive that I can achieve success in this interview. (Repeat this statement slowly and fully ten times in each exercise/practice, and before an interview.) My strengths include:

Here We Are Again - The Six Most Common Styles of Interviews

Repetition Works Wonders for Learning

There are as many styles and types of interviews as you have fingers and toes and more if you include deviations, modifications, and other such activities that interviewers may decide to use. I could produce an entire book on the interview processes and styles. However, this book is designed to aid you in managing your stress and anxiety in the job search, which includes the interview process as just one factor of that process. There are six most common styles or types of interviews that are generally used by interviewers. If you understand the complexities of these styles, you will be able to work your way around any stressful or difficult interview process you face.

Thea Kelly, author of "Get that Job! The Quick and Complete Guide to a Winning Interview," discusses twelve types of actual interview styles, but we will talk about the six most common. As an interviewing job seeker, you will most likely encounter six common interview styles. *As a job acquisition specialist, you will most likely encounter only six of these styles, unless your job is highly specialized and requires more than the normal job interview processes.* Therefore, this chapter will deal with these six common types. As a job seeker preparing for an interview, being prepared emotionally and informatively will be your greatest asset. Learning about and understanding the types of interviews you may face and practicing how to be successful in your mind's eye will provide you with confidence to overcome the stress that is built into the job interview process. Some job career specialists may also indicate a thirteenth style of job interview process being tested, and I will mention it here so you are aware, then return to the six common styles from which most styles of interview concepts originate.

The new thirteenth style of interview is designed to test your psychological behavioral and interspatial abilities. That sounds rather "scientific" and strange, but it has been used for engineers and other science-oriented individuals to test the "out of the box and conceptual thinking abilities" of job candidates. An employee, either the interviewer or an assistant, may escort you into a small, sparsely furnished office or room. On a table or desk may be some materials about the company, the job, a particular situation of the work, or something else. In this "hidden" style of interview, you are analyzed by your perceptions to the materials and items left within the room. You may be in this office for ten to fifteen minutes without seeing an interviewer or anyone else, or another individual may deliver additional materials while you wait. This "psychological" pre-interview period is designed to measure your ability to see if you are introspective to the point of just sitting on a chair waiting for the interviewer to come in, or taking some action with the materials left in the room. This interview style is designed to determine if you are able to fit comfortably into an uncomfortable situation. Will you be able to fit into a distinctly different corporate culture in a new job or a new company? Do you take action by yourself, such as investigating the materials in the room, and what do you do with the information you examine?

In addition, this style of "test" interview is to measure the candidate's ability to adapt to strange and unfamiliar situations, to view how a candidate can adjust to new or challenging cultures within a structure. Today's jobs are "gig"-oriented in a gig economy, which we will discuss in a later chapter, but this technique is a measurement to examine the adaptability of a candidate for today's short-term jobs.

As a job candidate, your job is to be proactive, to examine the materials left within this room or office. It is placed for a reason to measure your ability to seek out facts, learn about culture, and ask questions related to the materials you examined during the interview process. Simply stated, WILL YOU FIT into the culture of this organization or will you not?

Remember, all interviewers are charged with the task to examine how you as a job candidate deal with stress management! Stress management in the job interview process shows how you may deal with it on the job and how will it affect you in the hurry up, quick work environment of today.

The remainder of this chapter will be a very brief review of the less commonly used styles of job interviews so you become more acclimated to those styles and understand the stress that is deliberately inserted into each style. Effort will be placed on the six most common practices of interviews.

The Twelve Styles of Interviews That Can Produce Stress

In this section, I will highlight only those styles that are indicated with asterisks as they are the most commonly used.

1. The Phone Interview and Screening Out Process*
2. Face to Face or One on One at a Personal Interview*
3. Committee Interview, also known as the Panel Interview*
4. Group Interviews

5. Behavioral Interview, Testing your Reactions to Situations*
6. All Day/All Night Interview
7. The "Meal Time" Interview
8. Video Interviews*
9. Specific Case or Specific Job Structural Interview
10. "The Intentional Stress" Interview*
11. The Networking or Job Fair Interview*
12. Testing Interview

As a job seeker, you will most often find yourself in a telephone screening interview before any other type of interview first. Then, after you pass the first interrogation, you may find yourself in one or more face-to-face interviews, perhaps a panel or group interview and most likely the behavioral interview. In creative job interviewing processes, you may be asked to do a video interview. Although the current trend seems to be moving away from these "altruistic" styles of interviewing like the video interview due to personal security issues, you must be prepared for whatever is thrown your way. The pandemic of this year is increasing more interviewing online than any other reason. Regardless of what interview style you face, there will usually be more than one interview, and it will be one of the above mentioned styles.

The job interview type you face, regardless of whether it is a phone screening or stress interview, can be managed if you remember what was discussed in the beginning of this chapter and follow the rules and behaviors through each process. This requires practice and more practice, and the ability to listen and comprehend exactly about what is occurring during the interview process. As a job candidate, your ability to interact successfully in each type of interview increases your chance of advancing to the next step in the hiring process.

I like to emphasize my own 5P's Interviewing Behavior process, as a general set of rules for successfully managing any interview situation. Follow this guide and stress will be reduced for the interview process and with any interviewers. This "stress reduction process" for dealing with the stress during interviews will be more interactive with greater productivity and you will be on your way to your next job.

The 5 P's Process for Dealing with Stress in the Interview Process

Proactive behavior prevents – Poor performance – and Preparation prepares for Positive results and Planning produces great attitudes!

- **Proactive Behavior:**

As a job seeker, you must take the lead in controlling your message to the interviewer. Examine your thoughts and mindset, and compose those thoughts on paper how you want the interview process to progress from start to finish. List the steps you need to follow and make notes to use during the interview. This will keep you on track during the interview as the process is intentionally meant to "throw a curve ball or two at you." In addition, it will assist you in keeping you on message to the interviewer. So write out your plan from start to finish on how you want the interview to proceed, remembering that it may be in a slightly different order, but you can still control that order.

- **Poor Performance:**

Most candidates that are stressed during the interview process fail to plan anything about how the interview should flow. Have you tried to bake something and expect it to come out right without following a recipe? The same holds true for the interview process. The interviewer not only has a written set of notes and questions, i.e., his plans, but also a "check-off sheet" with items such as point values as you answer questions to evaluate you. The more points, the greater acknowledgement that your skills and experience are acceptable, and you will pass on to the next part of the process.

- **Preparation Prepares:**

As I just stated, I say that a lot don't I? Anyway, as I just stated, for the interview you must be ready for any "curveball," the baseball term you know. Okay, enough with the side track, and let's get back to the subject. When you prepare for differences or changes in the interview style, questions, or body language, you will be able to control the entire process to show yourself in a positive light. Your positive values to an employer become apparent and are reinforced.

An interviewer will on most occasions allow a candidate to present positive information more freely than negative. The more positive, the more the interviewer will listen; on the other hand, the more negative, the quicker the interview will terminate. When an interviewer wants to hear from you, the situational stress will be reduced, and you will have a clearer thinking process that will keep you on track.

Preparation is the key to this whole process. It is knowing about the job, the job requirements, and even the expectations of the employer. It is knowing the culture of the employer and if it matches with yours, and what will you accept or not accept. Do you want this job after your analysis of these factors prior to and after the interview?

As a job candidate, being positive brings out your skills, achievements, and attitude, and makes it easier to manage in a stressful situation, which is part of the measurement process of the interviewer.

- **Positive Results:**

Positive results are derived from the efforts of being proactive in your presentation. It is being prepared to maintain a positive attitude that you present during the interview regardless of the chaos that may be going on around you. It is not uncommon in the interview process for distractions to deliberately be presented to see how you handle these situations.

- ### **Planning Produces Great Attitudes:**

Every aspect of what you do to achieve a successful interview requires planning.

When I talk about planning, I talk about planning that is positive and reinforcing. It is the actions you put into the process: the interview process, the networking opportunity, your personal marketing portfolio, and every phase of the job acquisition process. If a job candidate has equal skills, experiences, and similar achievements, attitude will make the difference in the interview situation.

Attitude will assist the job seeker in being recognized! Interviewers are trained to make the interviewee feel uneasy and less confident, and to question themselves. Remember, attitude will establish your ability to fit into a new culture, accept diversity, and reduce onboarding time needed for a new employee. These are all a cost amount for any hiring manager in today's world of work.

What is the purpose of the interview?

1. The Telephone Screening Interview

This style of interview is common to almost 100% of job seekers, from the "blue collar" skilled worker to the senior executive of a multi-billion dollar corporation. This interview process is designed to screen any candidate out of the selection process with the discovery on even one minor flaw in work history, experience, social skills, attitude, or other points.

This interview process, which generally lasts from ten minutes to an hour, consists of human resources or even the hiring manager's administrative assistant asking questions to screen for the specific skill sets desired to meet the job criteria. Don't let this process fool you; in many cases, even the hiring manager has a less than 90% list of skills and experience that he is or she is seeking for the position. It is for this reason that the individual calling to initiate the telephone screening is to find a "zinger" response that will qualify or disqualify the candidate.

A "zinger" question is one that is asked to throw you a curveball to establish how you will answer a specific type of question and to see if you actually possess the skill sets the hiring manager has established for the "right" candidate. Most times the zinger question is NOT related specifically to the job, but to something tangential or completely off topic, all initiated to place the candidate off guard. It is usually a question that challenges the job seeker's analytical skills that will fit into the job requirements later in the interview process. Many recruiters will deliberately make them relevant to the job without you actually noticing the connection point. Finally, the **"zinger is designed to take you out of your comfort zone."** It is a question or statement that you may not have thought about in your preparation for the telephone interview. Take time to think about the question and how you will answer it for a few seconds before you place your foot in your mouth!

Thea Kelly[1], author of *The Quick and Complete Guide to a Winning Interview*, notes that "phone screening" is like a pop quiz, occurring when you least expect it. She states the necessity of not being caught off guard. It is important to be ready at any time with all your "personal marketing portfolio" information close at hand. Your primary concern is not to be stressed by failing to be prepared. However, that is easier said than done. Work with a friend who can contact you by phone for "practice." This will allow you to practice what behavior and activities you need to have set within your behavioral mindset when that call is received. Where will you have your materials and what phone will you use, i.e., the extension telephone in the house or your cell phone? Will any and all distractions be under control?

There is one point I want to be firm about. When the initial contact is made to establish a time for a phone interview, be proactive and polite, and with your own body and mind control, you can establish when the telephone screening will take place. When the time is near, have your notes and information easily at hand.

2. The Face-to-Face Interview & Online Interviews

The face-to-face interview is also referred to as the one-on-one interview. It is also the beginning of the sweaty palm, tight collar, stomachache, and slightly light-headed adventure. This is true only if you allow it to be such. Managing stress will minimize if not eliminate the stress that occurs during that time. If you are prepared in advance, you will prove your value to the interviewer within the first part of your meeting.

This style of interview is also referred to as the classic interview. The job candidate maybe interviewing with another HR representative or another individual who reports to the hiring manager. Don't be worried—remember this is an information-gathering session to see who you are, and your practice and emotional management will make you a winner.

The face-to-face interview is the most common style, next to the online "Zoom" interview used by employers today, and it may be the only style or a combined style with other parts of the interview process. This style is designed to allow you to tell your story, what you have to offer and why you are a value to the prospective employer. This is a show-and-tell time for presenting your achievements and accomplishments in a well-designed portfolio that highlights your skills, achievements, knowledge of what the employer is seeking and a single page listing in a distinct manner why this employer needs your skills and experience............YOU!

3. The Panel or Group Interview, AKA the "Inquisition" of all Interviewees

The panel or group interview is one in which the job candidate is interviewed by a multiple number of people. There may be members of the department in which the candidate will work or from across the organization. ***These types or styles of interview processes are designed to be stressful and even confusing with multiple interviewers are asking questions at the same time, or it may be organized with one person at a time asking a question.***

A group interview may even include more than one individual that is designed to add stress not only with the interviewers but also with multiple job candidates. There is a specific rationale for this interview style, and it is not necessarily an advantage for the interviewee. Candidates are placed together to see how they promote strengths and deal with socialization skillsets. The object is to establish how well a candidate can multitask with the competition and measure one candidate's answers against another's.

Your job is to establish a balance between control of your stress from the practice you have done and exchange information with the interview panel in an objective and non-stressed manner. Your objective is to promote your strengths, not express any negative comments toward another candidate, establish how you are able to work with others, understand diversity, and "fit" into the culture of the organization.

In many interviews of this style, the interview panel will have a check-off sheet to measure how the questions were answered via a scoring response and may even enable a confrontation between candidates. **Should this happen, LEAVE the room immediately. If a company acts in this manner during an interview, imagine how they will respond during the actual job.**

Key points in these interview styles include:

- The need for you to address all members of the panel or group utilizing eye contact, use a specific intonation of voice, stress your strengths, respond to questions only after you have taken a moment to formulate your response.
- Remember body language. Your body language is a key to your actual emotional and stress levels. Express confidence and relax no matter how questions are presented. Ask the interviewers to allow you to answer one question at a time if they attempt to ask multiple questions at one time.
- Control your stress, control your body language.

4. The Behavioral Interview

Over the last decade, the use of the behavioral interview style has become the most common, except for highly technical positions such as physicians, scientists, etc.

Over the last three decades, the use of the behavioral style of job interviewing has become the standard practice. It is used for positions that run the full gamut of job opportunities, including IT and other technical areas of specialties. This interview style is meant to be a process to establish in depth understanding of learned experience and how a candidate has "learned" from experiences, to achieve job success, in task management and accomplishments. The interview process is designed to examine how a job seeker's experiences were and will be prognosticators of success in the job.

There is a specific process used by interviewers in this process. Questions presented to candidates all seem to initiate within a set parameters of words or phrases. For example:

- "Tell me about a time when............"
- "What did you enjoy most about the challenges of your last position.........."
- "What was the most challenging aspect of your last few jobs.........."
- "How did you react, relate, develop a "teaming process," to do.........to accomplish a task..."
- "How did you or your team handle a failure...........with a particular task........"

These questions are a measurement of not only a candidate's experience and dealing with planning and intellectual processes but also an examination of a candidate's emotional maturity, as it pertains to business and challenging situations.

The primary difference between the question process in this style of interview is that the questions seek answers to behavioral reactions that utilized experience and emotional development. Not only are these questions seeking specific answers, but they seek an understanding of emotional development and diversity awareness within the workplace.

According to Carole Martin,[2] the use of keywords like "a time," "a failed task," "team planning," "time management," "describe a time," "describe a situation when," and similar words is common. The primary objective of a behavioral style interview is to "flush out details." It is designed so that an interviewer can obtain a more complete view of the work experience, emotional thought patterns, and emotional development of a candidate.

There is a specific technique to handle the stress and demands of a behavioral style of interview. This is done in two ways: one, through emotional understanding and second, through an answer process. Let's first examine how the stress of this interview style must be handled.

Emotionally, this style of interview along with the "stress interview" can be quite unnerving for a job seeker. It is for that reason that I have some simple ways to manage the stress before and during this style of interviews. These interviews are designed to produce stress and anxiety for any job seeker and the less prepared a candidate is for them, the more difficult they will be.

- Utilize the techniques that you have learned in the previous chapters on managing stress within the job search:

- Prepare a "cheat sheet" prior to any interview, especially in the situation where you may be facing a behavioral or stress interview.
- The "cheat sheet" is not a cheat sheet in the sense that you will have all the correct answers for the interviewers. It is a set of information that you can refer to when you need to answer questions.
- Examine your entire work history and volunteer work history and other sources of activities and events that could relate to work experiences. Prepare notes on the various successful experiences, somewhat successful experiences, and failed experiences. Note in this material how you solved the task, partially solved the task, what you might have accomplished in solving a task if you used a different method, and what you learned by failing a task.
- The objective is to have information noted to go back and refer to when asked a question. It also informs the interviewer the emotional intellect you possess or gained from past experiences. **Most of all, it reduces the stress you may have when determining how to answer those behavioral questions. There is nothing that shows more emotional intellect than having notes to refer to on what you learned or gained from those past experiences.** This shows preparedness for knowing your strengths, utilizing your strengths, and

overcoming stress while attempting to fumble around seeking an appropriate answer. You are prepared and stress free to continue on with the interview.

Now let's examine the other part of handling a behavioral style of interview. This is the process of using "storytelling." Storytelling is the process of answering the questioning by reciting a story of how you handled a particular situation in your work experiences or non-work experiences. **By having those experiences already in notes, it reduces the stress of trying to remember and compose a story.** Your job as a candidate is to explain to the interviewer(s) how you dealt with specific situations. Your answers should be presented in a structured way as a "well thought out story."

The most successful method is to answer the question by reciting an example of your work or non-work experiences in a formula. For example:

- Repeat the question the interviewer asked, confirming what the interviewer is actually asking.
- Initiate your "story" with the fact that you experienced this situation at XYZ company or ABC organization during a particular time.
- Explain the situational background, showing that you understand what was occurring in your job or other situation.
- Express in your story how you interpreted the

situation, relating to how it affected your job and yourself.
- Select in your answer a story that FITS the question asked. Don't use something made up. IF YOU HAVE NOT EXPERIENCED SUCH A SITUATION ASKED BY THE INTERVIEWER, YOU COULD PROVIDE HOW YOU BELIEVE SUCH A SITUATION SHOULD BE HANDLED. Remember, this could also be a situation that could not be resolved and the interviewer is determining how you handled the situation even if you failed or partially succeeded.

Remember, this style of interview process is a measurement of emotional thought patterns and emotional intelligence that is being examined, as well as job performance experience.

One final thought about this style of interview. The behavioral interview coincides with the "brand" you built about yourself. As a job seeker, you should have a well defined brand that represents your skills, abilities, accomplishments, and abilities to understand situations where you may have been successful, been partially successful, or failed. However, your brand needs to indicate you have the abilities to understand and seek success with tasks. Your brand here should be designed to show progressive development. Remember you initially presented your brand to a prospective employer in your resume, cover letter, or networking contact or connection. They should coincide with each other.

5. The Stress Interview

This style of interview process was prevalent from the 1970s through the beginning of the early 2000s. There are several industries and positions that continue to utilize this style, such as sales and marketing. The stress interview was slowly replaced by the behavioral style, although the stress interview is not entirely gone from the hiring process in one form or another.

This interview process was punctuated with questions and stressful situations to intimidate the candidate. The insurance industry still utilizes this process to some extent. Questions may be asked in harsh tones and demand immediate responses. In addition, the location of the interview may be held in multiple offices, including in restaurant situations. These behavioral situations are designed to intimidate the candidate to measure reactions to multiple situations. In some situations, the process is to promote doubts within the candidate that they are qualified for the position.

There are generally two ways to manipulate through this question process:

- Answer the interviewers' questions in a professional manner and then reply with a question directly related to the point that was raised. Here you show you have the necessary skills and experience and then by asking your own question, you are measuring the interviewers' understanding of those needs.

- Secondly, it is necessary to consider if the motives of the interviewers reflect how the company operates and what the organization's real philosophies are. In other words, do you want to be associated or employed by a company that maintains such a philosophy toward employees? Working for such an employer will add additional stress when you are again in the job search mode.

Just a final note about interview styles and stress. There continues to be a movement to utilizing more technology in the interview process. This includes the growing use of video interviews. Many employers are utilizing this medium to reduce costs, view a candidate in a home background environment, and in some cases, personal reasons.

- A video interview can seem intimidating, but if you are prepared, any unexpected situation will not take you off guard. Prepare an appropriate background within your location for the video interview, dress appropriately for the position you are being considered for, and continue through with the process. The key is preparation, preparation, and maintaining confidence.

A Generalized Outlook for Handling Most Styles of Stress Interviews

The most conflicting aspect to every interview situation is how to maneuver through each interview style. Most job seekers have an "inherent" fear of questions. Questions are a psychology method for many job candidates to accentuate a lack of skills or specific experience necessary to be selected for the position.

Job seekers need to accept that a nominal amount of fear is acceptable and normal during the process, although preparation in managing the stress produced makes it difficult to control and manage the stress and fear. To overcome stress, it is necessary to prepare a plan to control it and utilize that stress as a strength.

In handling any style of interview, the primary lesson is to learn and understand how to develop the necessary interview techniques: handling questions, atmosphere, establishing your goals, and promoting your strengths and capabilities. In addition, the necessity in the interview process to "read between the lines" or to recognize what the interviewer is asking and expecting.

Job search specialist, author, and speaker Carole Martin[3] notes there are many books on how to answer questions in the interview process. However, some are actually excellent and others concentrate on only answering questions. As she notes, "the problem is that you don't know what questions will actually be asked, or what the interviewer is seeking for an answer." In addition, many candidates do not know that it is acceptable to ask questions in return.

This may not be your fault, but the fact is, many interviewers are not trained in how to interview and have poor communication skill sets for the task. The art of answering a question is just that: an art. As an artist learns skills over time and through practice, this will apply to you by preparing for the process.

I stated earlier in this chapter that the most typical type of interview today is the behavioral style and can be more challenging than most of the other styles of interview processes. As a job seeker, it's imperative that you are prepared! It is something that I have repeatedly stated in this book. Planning and preparation are imperative and the key to success in each style of interview but most so with this behavioral style.

"Stories Again"

Earlier I discussed the need to develop and utilize stories to answer the questions that may be asked by the interviewer. These stories must be powerful, exposing your strengths and abilities, as well as your analytical skill sets. Stories or storytelling are most effective in the behavioral style of interviews and assists the candidate with promoting sound confidence and eliminating stress.

However, more than that, they must exude your confidence while answering questions. A well-established set of stories will bring "peace of mind" during the interview because you will be prepared for any type of situational question.

More on Successfully Handling the Behavioral Interview

I want to return to the handling of the behavioral style of interview. It has been noted that this is the most common style of interview process utilized today and can be stressful to many job seekers. The behavioral interview was designed to "predict the success" of a candidate. Many candidates fail to communicate and present themselves adequately and effectively during this style of interview.

You could ask, "How do you handle the behavioral interview process in a way that manages personal stress and improves performance?" As I stated previously, through planning and practice. As a job candidate, you must be able to decipher the difference between "generalized questions" and "direct probing questions." When you understand the meaning of the questions being asked and have practiced the appropriate answers, your stress will be minimized.

It is important to remember that in a behavioral style interview, it is necessary to utilize specific work history experiences and processes or interpersonal relationships. These experiences may be developed from successful experiences, your work performance, or failures. Your failures must show how you used organized and logical methods to solve problems. This is what an interviewer seeks. In addition, they may be related to your business methodology or psychological processes. Some of these may be:

- Can you give me an example of when or where or how [such and such a situation] occurred in your work experience?
- Tell me when you achieved…. How did you do it and why did you follow that process?
- Give me a time when your efforts failed to achieve the desired results. How did you process the steps you needed to follow? Where or at what point did you recognize that the actions you are taking would not work? Did you have or take the time to examine an alternative approach to the challenge?
- Your resume expresses continued success in all your endeavors. Is that completely accurate? Tell me more about that.
- How do you generally handle failure when assigned a specific task doing...?
- If you did not achieve success in a task, how did you mentally handle the end result? Did you stop at that point or do something different? Why did you take or not take such actions?
- Tell me about your greatest weakness and how it affects your process management of a task. What are some additional weaknesses and how does your work or psychological processes deal with such situations?

Many times a good interviewer will utilize additional questions to search deeper into your work processes on specific situations and even into your psychological processes. These may generally develop into somewhat stressful situations and are designed to measure your thought processes at that moment! Additional questions are valid to an interviewer to ascertain the validity of the answers you provide. Follow-up questions are asked also to measure the validity of previous questions in an interview as a measurement of accuracy of your answers.

All the questions mentioned here are secondary to the "killer of all questions." It's the "Tell Me About Yourself" question. I think every author on the topic of this question attempts to discuss the "best" or the "most appropriate" ways to answer this question. First, there is not one single way to answer this question, and yet many interviewees answer the question incorrectly. They simply get it wrong.

The main reason why an interviewer asks this question, or initially asks this question after a brief introduction, is to determine two very distinct qualities:

1. The interviewer wishes to determine if you are "listening." That is correct, listening to what is being asked. The interviewer is asking you about your work qualifications in general. This process is to determine if a candidate is able to "decipher" the code of the question. Approximately one half of inexperienced job seekers will answer this question by telling an interviewer their life story. The only

acceptable part of that an interviewer has interest in is how your "life experience" makes you a candidate qualified for a position.
2. Secondly, this question is designed to examine how your work history and experiences show skills necessary for the position you have applied for within the organization. This is the question you need to answer you need to answer carefully with the "story" of your work experiences, growth in responsibilities, successes, and objectives that you have developed before going into any interview.
3. The third item that an interviewer is seeking answers to is one that most candidates fail to understand. That is, can we afford this candidate? So what does that mean? This is a challenge, in that do you as a candidate understand the culture of the company and the ability to work effectively in a diverse cultural environment?

Successfully handling a behavioral style of interview is not difficult once you are prepared. Remember, every style of interview, especially this style, is a measurement of your core competencies:

- Adaptability
- Service – to client and organization
- Integrity and Trust
- Listening and Communication Skills
- Action – Solution Resolution
- Honesty and Integrity

- Problem Solving
- Initiative
- Leadership and Team
- Organizational Skillsets
- Result Oriented
- Self-Motivation
- Failure Planning
- Self-Evaluation

Preparation Method for Reducing Stress and Developing Your Story and Answers

In today's job search situation, there is no "I." In the workplace of today, companies and organizations are centered around teams, and a job candidate must understand that it is necessary to view yourself as "fitting into" the team. Although you are important, how you interact with the team in your previous work positions demonstrates your value of analytical skillsets and adaptability necessary for consideration by the interviewer.

How do you relate to the team without affecting your own values and accomplishments while maintaining low stress levels? It is vital to keep this point in mind. Of course this is an exercise requiring research, practice, and more practice. Determining the appropriate answer in the exercise will provide you with a response that meets the criteria of the interviewer and expresses your key necessity "to be that team player."

The form that follows, **ANALYTICAL INTERVIEW FORM**, is designed to assist you with developing the information necessary for the questions relating to "tell me about yourself." This form collects your experiences and provides you with a positive attitude and is designed to reduce stress as you prepare for the face to face time. Select four examples in each category as your base. You may expand it to as many examples as you would like, but select your most positive and successful experiences.

Analytical Interview Form:

1. Review your work history and list the situations that you worked within an "established team concept" or with just a "group" of other associates to successfully complete a project or task.

Work Example 1

Work Example 2

Work Example 3

Work Example 4

2. Now examine a specific role(s) or assignment(s) from your work experienced and develop what you successfully contributed to the group and the team effort.

Work Example 1

Work Example 2

Work Example 3

Work Example 4

3. Did your group, team, and yourself meet objectives? How did your work with these groups aid teams in achieving success? If the team, group, or you did not achieve complete success, where and what success did you bring to the team toward accomplishing what they did, how did your efforts aid the attempt or success, and if failed, how did you view the causes for failure and what more you could have accomplished to bring success?

Work Example 1

Work Example 2

Work Example 3

Work Example 4

4. What did you learn from your experiences, which included your successes, partial successes and failures? How will they assist your efforts in other jobs and tasks, and how did you come to these conclusions?

The form you completed is designed to assist you in how you "see" yourself as a vital job candidate. Take time to answer these questions and use them for interview preparation purposes. Remember, practice, practice, and practice.

How Do I View Myself Form Part 2

First, by examining how you performed as a team or group player as well as an individual, you are able to analyze the work each team or group member accomplished as a whole. However, you are also to examine your own contribution to the work project and develop a portfolio that will answer the concerns of specific information the interviewer requires.

Secondly, as I stated before, developing this information in advance and practicing the answers will significantly reduce stress and anxiety prior to and during any interview process.

Carol Martin[4] emphasizes in her book *What to Say in Every Job Interview*, there is no "I" alone in the interview process. I have already stated this throughout this book. This is the reason I suggest that you complete the previous exercise. Most job candidates forget to highlight the "I" in conjunction to how it is associated with the total work environment. As corporate business models continue to develop and hewn the "team concept" of project completion, it can be difficult to develop what you accomplished individually and how to associate that with teams or groups.

The following exercise takes the development of your skills, assets, and accomplishments to a more in-depth level of examination. It helps you establish a more rounded and refined way to view your skills, assets, accomplishments, and even failures. Take the time to really examine your work experiences before you answer the question on the next worksheet, **"How Do I View Myself?"** You may not like what you find or you may be quite satisfied. The objective is to establish more value in what you have and will bring to another employer.

As a job candidate, you may utilize this same worksheet for each of the jobs you held rather than your current or last position. The more time spent, the greater insight you will develop that will reduce stress and anxiety when confronted by the interviewer.

It is important to remember that you need to develop and utilize all your skills for the interview from past employment. Just as important is the acknowledgement of how some skills failed, what you learned, and how you would do the task again from what you learned.

This is what most interviewers and hiring managers are seeking.

When a job seeker is able to comfortably use this information, it brings greater stress reduction and exhibits confidence to the interviewer.

How Do I View Myself? Worksheet

1. As a member of a "team or group" assigned to accomplishing a task/project/assignment, can you recall the reasons/skills/accomplishments/activity history with each employer to explain why you were placed on that team or group?

2. Describe how your specific skills, accomplishments, analytical abilities, leadership strengths, or other abilities added value to a team's or group's success or failure? If your team or group failed, what part did you play and did you understand how to improve for the next project?

Complete this exercise for each relevant employer and job task as a team or group member. You may also complete this form if you were not on a specific team or group assigned to a task. Many employees fail to recognize that they may be on a team that is not designated as such but are grouped by the organization. Some examples of these types of teams would be sales on the regional, local, or even national level, or customer service such as in a company's customer service department. Although in these situations, you may not be assigned a specific project with a team or group, you are still measured under the same criteria and should be able to apply those skills, accomplishments, and lessons from past employers to the interviewer.

Finally I want to return to the key components that an interviewer seeks out during your face-to-face meeting. These key components should become and must become part of your story about "YOU" to the interviewer. During the interview process, understanding what is meant by each characteristic the interviewer seeks will reduce stress and anxiety. Carol Martin[5] lists many of the same key primary factors that your story must answer to successfully communicate to an interviewer. Understanding these characteristics will provide you an edge with the interviewer and aid in that "story" you want to express during the interview.

These characteristics include:

- **Honesty and Integrity** – These refer to yours

and the employer's moral issues that are expected in an employee.
- **Communication Capabilities** – Do you possess the ability to relate clearly to others, and express ideas succinctly and in a precise manner? In addition, are you able to define a process effectively for a win or lose experience?
- **Adaptability** – Are you open to change, and can you embrace change so the work environment can adapt to change that may occur rapidly?
- **Problem Solving** – The ability to analyze, evaluate, interpolate, utilize decision making and problem-solving methods.
- **Initiative** – Can you as an employee go above and beyond the normal, the unexpected? How resourceful can you be?
- **Leadership** – Are you a leader or follower, can you motivate others, are you a role model, are you able to accept being one in a team of several or many?
- **Plan and Organize** – Do you have experience in planning, being organized, delegating as necessary, and cooperating?
- **Accountable** – As an employee, are you results oriented and do you adapt from failures and learn from experience?
- **Composure** – How do you manage pressure, stress, anxiety, time management, and attitude?
- **Self-Motivated** – Will you be able accept

challenges? Are you enthusiastic, willing to accept challenges, and passionate about success?

There have been several skills and exercises discussed in this chapter to assist you as a job seeker. These exercises are presented to help you to reduce and manage stress and minimize anxiety. As a job seeker, following these steps will aid you in preparing for various types of interview styles and situational interviews.

Review these exercises on a regular basis and update the information you provided as you become more knowledgeable about your skills, abilities, and experiences. It is vital to remember to review these exercises prior to each interview.

8

WHAT'S NEXT AND HOW TO BE PREPARED FOR THE LONG & SHORT-TERM "GIG" ECONOMY

Since the term "gig economy" was first recognized around the Great Depression of 2008-2009 financial crisis, it has been noted in magazines, books, industry, and the general workforce of today. Task force labor has evolved and has become a significant factor in the overall economy.[1] The concept of creating short-term tasks has been around for a long time. Today, it has morphed into what we refer to as a very broad and encompassing set of workers who are full-time independent "contractors."

The term "gig" actually derived itself from the jargon of the jazz musicians as far back as the early 1900's. During the financial crisis of a few years past it took on a meaning of its own, referring to a workforce that is dedicated to generally short term, independent, mostly high-skilled workers who are hired to do work for corporations that would rather reduce costs than hire a full-time employee long term. As a choice you made, you are not a "gig" worker and it fits your needs, skillsets, and income requirements, for now at least. Well, you've done it, congratulations on your new employment. However, that is only your first step. Establishing a relationship for quality work and good reputation with clients is the beginning of the "yellow brick road." In the world of work today, we are in what is referred to as a "gig economy," regardless of what some "experts" wish not to call it. The gig economy began in 2008 and extended to current day, as jobs were beginning to return from the "Great Recession." This type of economy offered employment in a new and sometimes unfulfilling way, but it did offer reemployment.

This means that jobs are available ***for as long as an employer needs your services***. However, there are many workers who view this type of work as more satisfying than working for a single employer in or out of a brick-and-mortar location. Your survival is based upon your preparation, and this chapter will show you how to understand the gig economy and manage your current job and future employment opportunities. It will also offer some repeat steps to maintain a psychological balance as you face this new means of employment.

This chapter of the book will concentrate upon three specific areas: the rising trend in self-employment, how to acquire employment in the gig economy, and how to manage a career in the gig economy.

1. The new and current job.
2. Planning ahead, for your career or next job.
3. Managing stress and anxiety in the next job search.

This chapter will discuss for you several topics previously discussed in this book, but with the outlook of managing the gig economy. Many methods and techniques to reduce stress and anxiety in your current job search will still be viable for future job search adventures. These continuing methods will aid you to remain calmer, more focused and productive in your job hunt processes and everyday challenges. The preparation stages, including revising and modifying your personal marketing portfolio, employer examination, application process, including networking, interview process, rejection and finally success with your search will be easier, although just as challenging, as the last situation.

You will have a baseline of the proper materials necessary for the job search, greater confidence, in yourself and abilities, and a step above many other potential candidates. You will believe from the beginning you are the proper and outstanding candidate for the position you seek. Over the process of preparing emotionally you will find it easier to preparing your networking abilities, producing cover letters, revising your resumes to fit each opportunity and using your personal marketing portfolio to your best advantage. In some cases, the use of the traditional resume is no longer needed as a gig worker.

However, there are still some items that must be managed after your job search has succeeded to manage your new career. All of that centers around the new and continuing paradigm of work: "all jobs are temporary." The number of gig jobs continues to rise along with many advantages that workers feel about this type of work. These types of jobs are increasing in acceptance by multigenerational workers, as well as a loss of the old long-term single or even multi-employer workers.

What is the Gig Economy?

If you ever worked for Uber or Lyft, GrubHub or other such companies, you are a "gig worker." The gig economy is a labor market made up of mostly freelance or part-time workers who work a gig to supplement their income or when they desire. More gig workers are becoming full-time workers annually.

Today it's not that easy to join this labor market because jobs or gigs are decreasing, at least for the current and near future, due to the current pandemic facing the workforce. In other words, there are fewer gigs to fill than available workers seeking employment. Over the last decade the gig economy has provided millions of people with the ability to work independently and is projected to grow again and provide millions of additional jobs, although there are still many questions.

Although if you have been fortunate through your efforts to attain a gig job, it requires workers to be disciplined, as they must maintain their own schedule and act ultimately as their own "boss."

Okay, let's take a serious look at what the gig economy is. In a gig economy, temporary, flexible jobs are commonplace and companies tend toward hiring these independent contractors/freelancers instead of full-time employees. This practice undermines the need to maintain long-term employees and provide benefits that many companies deem as unnecessary expenses. In other words, the elimination of a lifetime career with a single employer.

- The gig economy is based on flexible, temporary, or freelance jobs, often involving connecting with clients or customers through an online platform.
- The objective of a gig economic workforce is to benefit workers by making work more adaptable to a worker, for business to provide flexibility as needed based on economic situations, and allowing greater adaptation to cyclical needs.
- ON THE OTHER HAND, the gig economy can have downsides due to the erosion of traditional economic relationships between workers, businesses, and clients.

Factors of a Gig Economy

Just to review, this nation's workforce is well on its way to establishing a well-entrenched gig workforce. Estimates are as high that as many as one-third of the workforce is already involved working in some gig capacity. Experts expect this number to rise as the types of positions facilitate independent "contractors" doing work that companies no longer need employees to come into as brick and mortar building to complete work tasks.

Employers also have a greater range of potential applicants to choose from, as they don't have to hire someone based on their proximity. Many jobs have been replaced or made more efficient by the use of more powerful computers and support personnel.

Even without the pandemic, in the modern digital world, it has become increasingly more common for people to work from home. Of course, employee costs are economic reasons why the development of the gig economy is so strong. As the economy in many business sectors continues to become more competitive, many employers cannot afford employees to do all the work that needs to be done, especially as benefit costs grow exponentially. So that business model has forced many employers to hire part-time or temporary employees for busier times or specific projects.

Critics of the Gig Economy Workforce

In lieu of the benefits of the gig worker and economy, there are several downsides to this gig economy. Again, the basic downsize of being a gig worker include:

1. A gig worker is NOT an employee of a corporation but rather an entrepreneur.
2. A gig worker does not receive normal corporate

benefits such as vacations, holiday pay, or other perks.
3. A gig worker's position can end at any time once a project is completed.
4. Gig workers must constantly network to continue to find work gigs.
5. As a gig worker, business expenses are not reimbursed by the client.

How Does the Gig Economy Work in Reality?

There can be found gig workers in almost every type of industry. As noted, most gig workers consist of performing smaller tasks and ancillary work that cannot be managed successfully in larger size organizations. Many gig workers can and do opt to work for a set number of hours, perhaps a specified shift that matches the corresponding work of the employer who has hired the worker. However, most of the hours and shifts are flexible. This is especially found to be realistic when a gig worker has a full-time job and is doing this "side" work after the normal work day schedule.

There are several misconceptions that are not generally noted in gig situations. Many people believe that gig workers are employees of the hiring organization. That is simply not the case! Many companies do not employ the gig worker; they simply utilize the services provided and pay an equal compensation for services rendered. You may know some of these companies as Uber, Lyft, Instacart, or TaskRabbitt.

It has been difficult to calculate the exact number of people working in the gig economy. This is due to the fact these workers are listed under several terms: freelancers, temporary workers, contractors, and others. According to the Bureau of Labor Statistics from the U.S. Government, as of May 2017, there were 10.6 million independent contractors whose could be classified as gig workers in one form or another.

In addition, figures have shown that the number of gig workers is divided quite evenly between men and women, but there are differences between what types of gigs they take on. Men are more likely to pursue labor gigs or high technology/information gigs, while women are more likely to strive for direct marketing positions and ancillary administrative support positions in Human Resources, Marketing, Operations, and Strategic Planning. As the need for gig workers increases, there is a greater mix between who pursues what type of position in the gig economy.

So why a chapter dedicated to the gig worker and gig economy? Simple: it's where jobs are heading for the next decade and maybe beyond. So now the question is how to survive and prosper in the gig economy. It takes planning, relationship and networking, skill development, and a well-designed business plan.

However, let me state this simple and realistic fact. Every worker needs to have a gig side income. A side gig job is a source of income as this economy continues to morph based on new growing markets and even pandemics. That's correct! Jobs with large corporations ARE GOING AWAY. Don't believe me, look at manufacturing sectors such as automotive, information technology production, consumer product goods, and the list goes on. These jobs may not disappear just here in the United States, but globally. Every employee needs to have a second source of income, whether they wish to believe it or NOT! Large, medium, and small manufacturing positions are on the decline. Information technology and artificial intelligence are replacing the human workforce in production, design, and planning operations too. Retail has seen declines as high as 45% nationwide in economic employment downturns. How do you think all this will affect you down your career path? Have you as a member of the workforce considered this loss of work impacting you and your family? To most Americans, it has not!

Preparing to Thrive in the Gig Economy......... The Real Story – Best Practices

"Thriving in the Gig Economy," an article by Gianiearo Petriglieri, Susan Ashford, and Amy Wrzesniewski,[2] states that the definition and characteristics of being part of the gig economy is in its infancy and still attempting to define itself. Although gig work has been around since the Great Recession of 2008, its definition actually continues to change.

These authors recognize that success in the gig economy derives from a balance between viability and vitality. It's easier than ever for companies in practically every sector to leverage the gig economy. Workers with a variety of skills at all levels can readily secure short-term gigs to earn or supplement a living, particularly by establishing a plan based around the following criteria.

Developing Yourself as a Gig Worker in A Positive Way

1. Find Your Niche Utilize your existing skills and interests, but also follow your passions. Following your passions will lead to a positive attitude and greater opportunities.

2. Leverage Technology Platforms It is important to identify what you desire to focus upon, in other words, the type of work you're interested in acquire additional training and connect with groups who can support your objectives. Finding others who share similar interests will aid in connecting you with clients who can utilize your skill sets. Developing these connections with groups make it easier to secure temporary work without the time consuming task of seeking out clients on your own. Remember you want to reduce stress in every manner possible.

3. Establish Working Schedules As with any business or project, proper planning is vital for success. Although as a gig worker the greatest benefit may be flexibility, determining your work availability ahead of time makes it easier, so select profitable gigs that will lead to more successful ventures. Establishing will prevent the possibilities of forcing changes at the last minute to your schedule and aid in building long term client relationships. Commitments are vital as a gig worker and clients measure your value by your commitment.

4. Managing Your Finances Whether you are a small business or major corporation finance management is crucial for success. As a gig worker, developing a budget, organizing your finances, and planning for taxes and other contingencies are vital for success.

Many gig workers will develop a budget for each project to manage expenses and to manage profits and expenses per gig and compare those figures at the end of the fiscal period. This is most helpful during tax preparation time, which is actually a full-year project.

5. Every Gig is an Audition Give every gig job your all, no if ands or buts about it. Even if you are employed for a single task/operation/shift for some company. Remember, as with any corporation of any size, there is a "feedback loop" that allow employers to rate the performance of a gig worker. How you are rated can determine your success as a gig worker and gaining more new clients. Even if there is no formal feedback loop system in place, your reputation is key to your success, and exceeding expectations can earn you referrals and recommendations.

The gig economy, especially of 2020, offers abundant opportunities for the workplace and employers who have specially needed skillsets.

There are multiple basic numbers that account for gig workers today, and they will show the workforce just how valued the gig worker is to the success of business. Since the number of gig workers is huge, you will find a wide range of variances in numbers.

One study by MBO Partners denotes a person working over 15 hours a week who chose this particular mode of work and doesn't plan on altering it is considered a full-time gig worker. Whereas, according to a report by the McKinsey Organization, any gig worker who earns their primary income as a gig worker is full-time invested in gig work. According to Upwork, by 2027 there will be 86.5 million freelance workers, a significant growth from just 2018. Gallop Polls indicate that 36% of workers participate in the gig economy through either their primary or secondary jobs. Meanwhile, Edison Research states that 44% of workers in the gig economy use this income as their primary financial resource.

Other more interesting facts about gig workers include:

- For 53% of gig workers aged 18-34, according to Edison Research, gig work is their primary source of income.
- In addition, most gig workers are in the younger age group of 18-34, according to Edison Research.
- 1 in 6 workers in traditional jobs would like to become a primary independent earner, according to the report by McKinsey.

LIVING AND SURVIVING PANDEMICS, RECESSIONS, AND OTHER ECONOMIC CHAOS

Throughout the last eight chapters of this book, I discussed methods and techniques for navigating a successful job search by managing stress, anxiety, and the utilization of the most up-to-date techniques for your job hunt. Chapters 1 – 8 covered topics that included:

- How Attitude, Stress and Anxiety impact your successful job search.
- There were several individual chapters on the best way to understand stress, anxiety, and how to handle it during the job search and the job interview process.
- Third, there was a discussion on the effective and successful use of Time Management in your job search.
- The following chapter reviewed in depth the

elements of Effective Communication for interviews, networking, and your job search.
- The Personal Marketing Portfolio and its value were discussed to give you as a job candidate an edge over the competition.
- The remaining chapters handled areas that dealt with positive tools for your job search.
- Chapter 8 highlighted the greatest change in jobs today, the "gig economy."
- Finally, this last chapter is a review of what a job seeker will always need to have in his or her bag of tricks for the successful job hunt when times are not so good.

This chapter is designed to bring all the rest of the information, neatly, concisely, and in a way to aid you when the stress, anxiety, and other factors get to you. These are current topics still strongly needed to be understood and utilized in today's job safari.

Don't Forget What Employers Still Seek When Searching for Quality Employees; the Challenges Between Gig and Company-Hired Employees

As a job seeker,[1] it is vital to remember to always view the current position's duties and responsibilities from the company's perspective. Most hiring managers have a generalized "picture" of who they seek, what skills they want, and whether that individual will be an employee or a "gig worker." Regardless, whether an employer is hiring an employee or a gig worker, there are specific requirements that job candidates must continue to maintain.

Are you a self-motivated individual? Company employees and gig workers must justify that they manifest this behavior. An employee will continue to want to talk about that in your interview as a gig worker or company employee. Remember to use stories to express how you are motivated and whether you are hired as an employee or gig worker.

Are you organized? Employers, whomever they hire, require employees who are extremely organized and can prove they will successfully manage a project to completion. Highlight these points to them, how you utilize them, and how they are part of your success package.

Do you have experience working remotely for a few weeks or as part of your current role? Do you understand the challenges required as a gig worker for this type of employment or due to some unforeseen circumstances? It is imperative to highlight this for all your work experience. In this area, point out key processes and success factors achieved. Be sure you can fit them into situations working for a company, as well as a gig worker.

Remember, the objective of all these points is to reinforce the skills needed and your personal marketing for employment as a corporate hired worker or as a gig worker. They are transferable things a job seeker must understand. [2]

In addition, technological skill sets are something all employers are seeking in greater quantity than ever! If you are working for a company, you will find support easier from the IT staff, but as a gig worker YOU must have the owned skills necessary to carry out the job requirements and additional training may be required. In today's fast changing economic world, a worker must be able to change direction on a dime. This means sharpening your skills so that no matter whom you are working for, you can adapt quickly. Remember these tech skills can run the gamut from understanding the use and value of online interviews and meetings to understanding and implementing specialized software.

Some significant sources of knowledge can be gained through utilizing videos and training courses by online locations including:

- Udemy
- Coursera
- You Tube
- Kahn Academy

And there are many others that specialize in specific types of training.

There are hundreds of companies and sectors that are still hiring employees, but the list of gig job employers continues to outpace others in some areas. According to the website Flexjobs, there are some top companies that gig workers should seek out.[3]

Writer Brie Reynolds lists dozens of companies, taken from a database of FlexJobs's study on clients and non-clients, as great sources for employment for gig and non-gig workers. These firms hire full- and part-time employees for gig work from home. FlexJobs is a subscription service for job seekers that features flexible and remote jobs. With an A+ rating from the Better Business Bureau, it allows various industry sectors to fully vet the accuracy of their information and jobs listed, ensuring that customers have a safe and positive job searching experience. It is an excellent tool for many job search boards.

Older, Newer, and Reawakened Methods Used for Finding Jobs Still Work

Remember at the beginning of this book, I stated it was written to deal with the stress and anxiety of the job search and how to manage these situations. Stress and anxiety is the job seeker killer!

However, as a job seeker, there are several ways to seek employment that are still valid. These are common and old practices that have never really disappeared from the job search. Some of these processes include using job boards and determining how companies leverage potential employees to hire, which are still valid and demand a note before I close this book.

Employers don't like to hire incompetent employees. Most employers don't relish the use of job postings as their favorite way to seek out candidates. Companies know from experience that a "bad" hire, someone who does not fit in or can't do the job well, is an unnecessary expense, can cause damage to the organizational functions, and may cost more to fix than just capital expenses. Of course, employers prefer hiring methods that produce good results. This means finding a candidate who has good skills, fits into the organization's culture, and has previous experience.

Countless studies over the years have shown several methods still function well for the job search:

- **Internal transfer.** Obviously you will need to be an existing employee for this method to work, but it is a much lower risk than an internal hire. Internal transfers know the internal and external rhythms of the company compared to an outsider. Also searching for internal positions is generally more "locatable" than if one was not within the company.
- **Employee Referral.** This has always been an old-time favorite way of hiring for somebody who already doesn't work in the organization. In this method, friends are able to connect with friends about available positions and use contacts to get past the gatekeeper.

Other Highly Valuable and Older and Current Ways to Finding a Job Without Using Job Boards

1. **Spend as much or preferably more time on LinkedIn as you spend on Job Boards.** LinkedIn is noted as the hang out place for

recruiters. Finding qualified candidates on LinkedIn is more efficient for them than trying to find just anyone, but the most qualified of the qualified candidates of the large number of job applications that are received. Recruiters hunting LinkedIn are seeking "All Star" matched with the specific keywords.

2. **Reach out to old friends.** They can be inside or outside of LinkedIn or other Social Media outlets. Catch up with them and what is happening in their live. Ask for introductions, referrals and additional contacts. Here you can even leverage Employee Referral Programs. Perhaps that old contact will receive a bonus for finding your talent.

3. **Consider becoming a "boomerang" employee.** A "boomerang employee" is someone who worked for a company, decided to leave, and wants to be reemployed. There is or was something that the employee liked while serving that employer.

4. **Join an existing job club or reform one.** Job seekers are on the increase. Job clubs present excellent opportunities to share values, opportunities, and experiences. Job clubs provide a support network, and you will need a support network during this time. Job clubs present speakers and information relating to the job search for today, what local and other employers seek, and opportunities that are available.

5. **Take a class or some training.** Learning

should and will help increase knowledge and skills, and may certainly expand your network!

6. **Accept part-time or temporary work.** This is a great way to generate income and even build your network. Sometimes these types of jobs are posted as temp to perm.

7. **If you like to write, write.** Many job seekers have vast amounts of knowledge in which employers would "give their eye teeth for." Writing makes you known and increases your chance of being recognized. It assists in making you a <u>visible expert in your field</u>!

NOTES

1. How Attitude, Stress and Anxiety Impact Your Job Search

1. Peter Voight, Senior Contributing Editor, Monster.com, page accessed September 2, 2013.
2. Elizabeth Scott, MS, Ask.com referenced 9/2013, reference to Stress Management in what is
    referred to by this author as Reframing.
3. Alex Groberman, Difference Between Stress and Anxiety, 2011

2. Attitude: How to Define, Build, and Manage it for the Job Search

1. Eli Andur, Career Coach, Author, Adjunct Professor, Farleigh Dickenson University
2. John C. Maxwell, author, speaker, Leadership Expert.
3. Dr. Wayne Dyer, PhD, author, speaker.
4. Dr Dwayne Dyer, PhD, author, lecturer, behaviorist.
5. John C. Maxwell, *The Difference Maker*, author, motivation specialist, speaker.
6. John C. Maxwell, *The Difference Maker*.
7. John C. Maxwell, "The Difference Maker", author, speaker, motivational and business
    specialist. Thomas Nelson, 2006
8. Rhonda Byrne, The Secret, The Secret, Alrea Books, 2006
9. John C. Maxwell, "The Difference Maker," Thomas Nelson Inc., 2006

3. Stress: How to Manage it in the Job Search

1. Aneta Peng, Researcher for the Five O'clock Club
2. H. Norman Wright, A Better Way to Think, 2011
3. Archibald Hart, Habits of the Mind, Dallas: Word, 1996
4. S. Nolan-Hoekssma and C. Davis, "Thanks for Sharing That: Ruminators and Their Social
   Support Networks," *Journal of Personality and Social Psychology* 1999.

4. Managing Time and Controlling Stress Factors

1. Dirk Zeller, *Time Management for Dummies, Mini Edition*, 2013.
2. Dirk Zeller, *The Time Management for Dummies, Mini Edition*, 2013.
3. Mary Eileen Williams, MS, "Land the Job You Love-10 Surefire Stratagies for Jobseekers
   over 50."
4. Joseph Newberger, Worktree.com, "Tips to Minimize Job Hunting Stress," accessed June 2014.
5. Dr. Richard Bayer, COO, The Five O'Clock Club, author *The Good Person Guidebook;*
   Transforming your Personal Life, 2008.

5. Effective Communication in the Job Search

1. Mike Bechtle, author, communications specialist, speaker, *How to Communicate with*
   Confidence, 2008.
2. Mike Bechtle, author, *How to Communicate with Confidence*, 2008.
3. Mike Bechle, author, speaker, *How to Communicate with Confidence*, 2008.
4. Mike Bechtle, author, speaker, *How to Communicate with Confidence*, 2008.

6. Developing a Positive Marketing

1. Laura DeCarlo, *Resumes for Dummies, 7th Edition,* 2015, John Wiley and Sons.
2. "Overwhelming Majority of Companies Say Soft Skills are Just as Important as Hard Skills,"
    Harris Poll study on behalf of CareerBuilder, April 10, 2014.
3. Louise Kursmark, Author, *"Modernize Your Job Search Letters: Get Noticed......Get Hired";*
    Nov. 2016; Career Consultant, Executive Resume Writer, and Career Consultant, LinkedIn.
    article culled 1/11/2017.
4. Laura DeCarlo, *Resumes for Dummies,* 7th ed., 2015. John Wiley & Sons, Inc.
5. Robyn Schlinger, Robyn's Resumes, www.robynresume.com, author, accessed 8/2020.
6. jobscan.co/resume-templates, samples modified and accessed 8/20/2020.
7. jobscan.co/resume-templates, samples modified and accessed 8/20/2020.
8. jobscan.co/resume-templates, samples modified and accessed 8/20/2020

7. Positive Tools, Methods, and Techniques for a Productive and Positive Interview Experience

1. Thea Kelly, author of *The Quick and Complete Guide to a Winning Interview,* and career specialist.
2. Carole Martin, "What to say in every job interview, there is no I in interview."
3. Carole Martin, "What to Say in Every Type of Interview......", author, speaker and noted job
    search specialist.
4. Carol Martin, *What to Say In Every Interview* author.
5. Carole Martin, *What to Say in Every Job Interview,* author, speaker.

8. What's Next and How to be Prepared for the Long & Short-Term "Gig" Economy

1. John Frazer, How the Gig Economy is Reshaping Careers for the Next Generation; accessed
    forbes.com, 8/31.2020, author.
2. Gianpiero Petriglieri, Susan J. Ashford, Amy Wrzesniewski, "Thriving in the Gig Economy,"
    Diversity Latest Magazine, Popular Topics Podcasts, April 2018.

9. Living and Surviving Pandemics, Recessions, And Other Economic Chaos

1. Susan P. Joyce, editor and publisher of "WorkCoachCafe," Publisher of Job-Hunt.org,
    columnist on Huffington Post and writer for LinkedIn.
2. Deanna deBara, freelance writer, Portland, Oregon, 2020.
3. Brie Weiler Reynolds, Career Development Manager, 2020.

www.ingramcontent.com/pod-product-compliance
Lightning Source LLC
LaVergne TN
LVHW051517070426
835507LV00023B/3154